Revised & Expanded
Apostolic Authority, Every Believer's Privilege

Living In Kingdom Authority

Every Believer's Privilege

By Martin Schmaltz, D.C.

Apostolic Missions Inc.

Copyright © 2012 Martin Schmaltz

ALL RIGHTS RESERVED

No portion of this publication may be reproduced, stored in any electronic system or transmitted in any form or by any means, electronic, mechanical, photocopy, recording, or otherwise, without the written permission from the author. Brief quotations may be used in literary reviews.

This book is sold for information purposes only. Neither the author nor the publisher assumes any responsibility for the use or misuse of information contained in this book. Although the author and publisher have made every effort to ensure the accuracy and completeness of information contained in this book, we assume no responsibility for errors, inaccuracies, omissions, or any inconsistency herein. Any slight of people or organizations are unintentional.

Printed in the United States of America

ISBN 978-0-9845503-1-9

Unless otherwise indicated, all Scripture quotations are taken from the King James Version.

For information contact us:
www.martinschmaltz.com
maschmaltz@juno.com

Dedication

Living In Kingdom Authority is dedicated to Jesus Christ. He truly is my source.

To Ava, my wife, companion, and partner in ministry.

Preface

It has been over six years since the Lord inspired me to write *Apostolic Authority, Every Believer's Privilege*. During these years, I have been privileged to minister these principles in many different meetings, both in the U.S. and foreign lands. In each case, the Lord has not failed to confirm His word with miracles of healing and empowerment of the believers.

Along the way, these experiences and further study have led me to write this new edition with a new title: *Living In Kingdom Authority*. While some of the material will be familiar to readers of the original version, there is approximately 50% new material in this book. There are new chapters such as: *The Kingdom Is His Plan, Your Resources & Kingdom Authority, Makin' It Real and His Word Confirmed*. Also, a greater depth of understanding regarding the idea of image and glory has resulted in expansion of the original first few chapters.

Finally, I have chosen to change the title for a couple of reasons. First - *Living In Kingdom Authority* is more appropriate to God's plan for us. Second - the term apostolic is actually a confusing one in the church world. Many have preconceived ideas regarding this term. I believe it has been some of these ideas that have actually kept people from pursuing the truths presented.

I trust, whether you are a first time reader or a returning one, you will find *Living In Kingdom Authority* an inspiring faith builder.

Yours for His Kingdom,
Martin Schmaltz, D.C.

CONTENTS

Introduction

CHAPTER 1	The Kingdom Is His Plan	1
CHAPTER 2	The Glory Of The Kingdom	9
CHAPTER 3	In His Image	19
CHAPTER 4	The Real Apostolics	29
CHAPTER 5	Your Place Of Authority	41
CHAPTER 6	Developing Kingdom Thinking	53
CHAPTER 7	Demonstrating Kingdom Authority	61
CHAPTER 8	The Kingdom Model Of Discipleship	73
CHAPTER 9	Your Resources & Kingdom Authority	85
CHAPTER 10	The Stronghold Of Religious Tradition	95
CHAPTER 11	Makin' It Real	105
CHAPTER 12	His Word Confirmed	115
Conclusion		121

INTRODUCTION

The young woman lay on a pallet of blankets. The muscles of her extremities were withered so that her legs and arms were drawn up towards her torso in an agonized, twisted position. The little strength she possessed only allowed her the ability to lift and turn her head. As she turned towards me with a pleading look in her large, sorrow-filled eyes, the Spirit spoke to me and said, "A withered spirit."

This vision occurred one morning in prayer, as I sought the Lord for His purpose and direction. With this statement, came the understanding that the church possessed a withered spirit. The spiritual muscles had atrophied to the place that there was no longer strength to move or minister. The withering had produced a helpless body; unable to fulfill the purpose it was created for.

From my college days and years in practice, I know that in the human body muscles will begin to waste away, losing both size and strength primarily for two reasons. First, there is an injury or disease to the muscle itself. Secondly, the muscle has lost its nerve communication with the brain. Both of these, if untreated, will result in progressive loss of strength and ability of the muscle. Likewise, we find that individuals and churches begin to waste away, loosing their spiritual strength for similar reasons. They have experienced an injury or there is a loss of communication with the Spirit of God. Ultimately we find a withered, weak and powerless church, lacking the ability to exercise Kingdom authority or dominion.

The purpose of this book, *Living In Kingdom Authority*, is to share with the church what the Lord has revealed in regards to His desire for us to walk in dominion and authority. When looking at the first church, authority and power were demonstrated on a consistent basis. Just as Jesus came teaching, preaching, healing all manner of diseases and casting out demons, His early church continued in the same ministry. Wherever the disciples went preaching, the Lord confirmed their word with signs and wonders. The power of God was evident in the daily lives of the first believers, so much so that they were said to have *"turned their world upside down."*

However, the 21st century church is withered. There is very little manifestation of Kingdom power in the lives of believers. We have reached the place that some leadership states that this type of miraculous demonstration was only for the establishing of the first church and is not necessary today. I submit, however, that we have come to the place, much like the Pharisees of Jesus day, that we teach the traditions of men or organizations; thereby making the commandments of God powerless. The result is that we have lost the ability and faith to walk in Kingdom authority.

Living In Kingdom Authority is about reclaiming what the Lord desires for His people. It is about understanding the authority we have been given to demonstrate God's power. It is grasping what it means to be sent, and how to operate in our sentness. It is about exercising the dominion that was given to Adam in the beginning. It is about you and I fulfilling, with ultimate authority and power, His purpose for our individual lives.

My desire is that somehow in the following pages, the Lord will use these words to birth in you the vision of *Living In Kingdom Authority* and His desire to demonstrate Himself through you.

Yours for His Harvest
Martin Schmaltz, D.C.

CHAPTER 1
THE KINGDOM IS HIS PLAN

The doctrine of the Kingdom of Heaven, which was the main teaching of Jesus, is certainly one of the most revolutionary doctrines that ever stirred and changed human thought. ~ H G Wells

Since we are going to delve into living in Kingdom authority, we should lay the foundation of what the Kingdom is. This chapter is not meant to be an exhaustive study, but to give us a context or framework of God's kingdom perspective. Grasping an understanding of the Kingdom will transform our concepts of the church, its purpose and our individual involvement.

It is interesting to note that Jesus' inaugural message was very pointed about one thing: *"Repent, for the kingdom of heaven is at hand" (Matthew 4:17).* Mark's version quotes Jesus as saying: *"The time has come...The kingdom of God is near. Repent and believe the good news!" (Mark 1:15).* The implication of this statement is that there was a time line of Kingdom manifestation and its appearance was the good news, or the Gospel.

So, What Is The Kingdom?

Since Jesus placed such significance on the arrival of the Kingdom, it prompts the question "What is the Kingdom and it's importance?"

In the previously above quoted texts, the Greek word translated kingdom is *basileia* and means *"sovereignty, royal power, dominion,"* (Vine's). It also can mean *"rule, or a realm"* (Strong's) and can be translated as reign. So Jesus was saying that the power, dominion or rule of heaven was at hand. Or it could be stated the realm or reign of God was at hand. Further, the English word kingdom is said to be derived from two words; *"king - meaning head of a kin"* and *"dom - meaning state, condition or power, position of domain."* Or it could be stated: *"kings domain."* It is the territory or area over which a king reigns and rules. Therefore, the Kingdom is the reign or rule of God, whether in heaven or on earth. It is the place where His dominion or power is expressed. It is also the purpose or intent for the extension of his rule or reign.

In view of the above, Jesus' proclamation in Matthew 4:17 was an introduction that the dominion or rule of God had come near. This declaration was of great spiritual, prophetic and cultural significance for His intended audience. To the Jewish people, the idea of the Kingdom was a prophetic fulfillment linked with the Messiah. Their concept of messianic deliverance was not an escapist view of a far away place called heaven: It was packaged in the idea of Kingdom restoration. Thus Jesus' statement carried profound revelation and signified a major step in God's prophetic timeline.

The Kingdom IS His Plan

To grasp the truth of the Kingdom, we must put it in proper context. **It is not part of God's plan: it IS His plan!** I cannot emphasize this too much! The Kingdom theme can be traced through the word of God, from the creation story of Genesis to the book of Revelation. The Kingdom was not intended as a one-time event or just an Old Testament governmental structure: it has been in the mind of God for eternity. The psalmist tells us: *"Thy kingdom is an everlasting kingdom, and thy dominion endureth throughout all generations" (Psalms 145:13)*. Daniel stated to King Nebuchadnezzar that God's Kingdom was *"an everlasting kingdom, and his dominion is from generation to generation" (Daniel 4:3)*. Regarding Jesus, the angel Gabriel spoke to Mary stating that God would give to him David's throne and *"he shall reign over the house of Jacob for ever; and of his kingdom there shall be no end" (Luke 1:32-33)*. The Kingdom IS His plan!

Not only is His kingdom an everlasting one, but also the saints are to have an active part in its manifestation. Again, the psalmist tells us that they will *"speak of the glory of thy kingdom, and talk of thy power; To make known to the sons of men his mighty acts, and the glorious majesty of his kingdom" (Psalms 145:10-12)*. Daniel weighs in again prophetically and tells us that the saints will take the Kingdom and posses it *"for ever, even for ever and ever" (Daniel 7:18)*. Further on, we will elaborate more on the saints or church's involvement, but suffice it to say we are to play an integral part in His kingdom manifestation. Yes, The Kingdom IS His plan!

The Kingdom Established

From the first verses of Genesis, we see God's plan unfold. Understanding that the Kingdom is where the reign, domain or dominion of God exists, gives us the context to view its establishment in the creation process.

As part of the process, God created Adam in a special way for a unique purpose. What set Adam apart from the rest of creation was his being in the image and likeness of God. With this distinction, he was given dominion and rule over creation. It was through Adam, God planned to manifest Himself and reign over creation. If Adam were to obey the command to be fruitful and fill the earth, it would be by the propagation of mankind, God's image and dominion would be established throughout the earth. (We will elaborate in chapters two and three). Unfortunately, because of disobedience, Adam and his offspring lost the right and ability to demonstrate God's dominion. From that time on, we see God working to reestablish his domain (kingdom) on the earth.

Israel, God's Kingdom Demonstration

We now fast-forward many centuries to God's next manifestation of His kingdom, this time in the nation of Israel. After delivering Israel from Egypt, God, via Moses reveals his purpose for them: *"And you will be my kingdom of priests, my holy nation" (Exodus 19:6).* It was God's intent that living under his theocracy, revealing a distinct culture, they would be His instruments on earth to demonstrate His reign. It was this Kingdom (dominion/reign) that would be the method of revelation to the nations of God's identity.

Much like Adam and Eve, Israel did not always provide the best demonstration of God's kingdom. Yet, because the Kingdom IS His plan, we see God continuing to bring about Kingdom restoration. His next step: the Kingdom of God in Jesus Christ.

Jesus Ushered In The Kingdom

With his ministry, Jesus steps on the scene as the ultimate manifestation of God and his rule. As previously stated, his first message centered on the Good News (Gospel) that the Kingdom was here. However, not only did he declare the Kingdom's presence, he stepped it up a notch and demonstrated the power and dominion of the Kingdom like none other. Matthew, in his gospel tells us *"Jesus went about all Galilee, teaching in their synagogues, and preaching the gospel of the kingdom, and healing all manner of sickness and all manner of disease among the people" (Matthew 4:23).* I believe the miracles performed by Jesus were to reveal the presence of the dominion of His kingdom. In fact, when the source of his miraculous power was attributed to Beelzebub, Jesus responded with this statement: *"if I cast out devils by the Spirit of God, then the kingdom of God is come unto you" (Matthew 12:28).* He was clearly declaring that the miracles he performed were the proof that the Kingdom of God had come to earth.

The Kingdom And His Church

Unfortunately, again Israel did not grasp the significance of their purpose as God's kingdom people. Their crucifixion of Jesus resulted in the Kingdom demonstration being transferred to a new nation or people group, the New Testament church. Jesus used the Parable of the Tenants *(Matthew 21:33-42)* to illustrate Israel's rejection of himself and the Kingdom, followed by a prophetical statement: *"The kingdom of God shall be taken from you, and given to a nation bringing forth the fruits thereof" (Matthew 21:42).* The Jewish people had such a nationalistic concept of the Kingdom of God; they rejected their King *(Matthew 26-27).* It is a sad commentary that they did not learn the lessons of history.

In his first letter, Peter gives further clarification to the church regarding their Kingdom role. He states, *"But you are a chosen race, a royal priesthood, a holy nation, a people for his own possession, that you may proclaim the excellencies of him who called you out of darkness into his marvelous light" (1 Peter 2:9 ESV).* In this text, the word *"royal"* is *basileios* and means *"royal, kingly or regal"* (Thayer's). So it could be stated we are a kingly priesthood, obviously then, we must be associated with a kingdom.

It is interesting to note the obvious similarities in verbiage used by Peter and God's calling of Israel in Exodus 19:5-6 when he called them to Kingdom manifestation. Remember God referred to them as His possession, a kingdom of priests and a holy nation. It is no coincidence: both were called to be His kingdom representatives.

It is now God's intent that through Jesus Christ, the church is the vehicle of Kingdom demonstration. As born again believers, we are the representatives of the King and His kingdom.

You And His Kingdom

It is wonderful to know that God has chosen to manifest his Kingdom plan today through his church. But to me, the greater wonder is to grasp that we, not buildings or organizations, are the church commissioned to demonstrate His kingdom. It is a personal thing!

In a dialogue between Jesus and Nicodemus, a religious leader of his time, we are presented the method of our access to the Kingdom. Jesus stated:

> *"Verily, verily, I say unto thee, Except a man be born again, he cannot see the kingdom of God" (John 3:3)*
>
> *"Verily, verily, I say unto thee, Except a man be born of water and of the Spirit, he cannot enter into the kingdom of God" (John 3:5)*

Jesus' statements clearly tell us that our new birth experience not only allows us to see the Kingdom, but also allows us to enter into the Kingdom. It is at our born again experience we change citizenship from the kingdom of darkness into God's kingdom.

Paul references this transference of kingdoms when writing to the church at Colossi stating: *"Who hath delivered us from the power of darkness, and hath translated us into the kingdom of his dear Son" (Colossians 1:13).* The Greek word used for "translated" is *methistemi* and means: *"to transpose, transfer, remove from one place to another: change of situation or place"* (Thayer's). The New Living Translation puts it this way: *"he has brought us into the Kingdom of his dear Son."* Paul is further elaborating that we have been transferred or moved from the kingdom of darkness to the Kingdom of Jesus. This is a present active event, not something we are waiting for.

To the church at Thessalonica, Paul states that we have been called into His kingdom and glory. He states: *"That ye would walk worthy of God, who hath called you unto his kingdom and glory" (1 Thessalonians 2:12).* The word *"called"* here is *kaleo* and it means, *"to call anyone, invite or summon"* (Vine's). The word unto in the original is *"eis"* and means *"to or into (indicating the point reached or entered), of place, time"* (Strong's). So Paul is saying we have been invited or summoned to **a particular place**, that being the Kingdom!

Finally, while we have been invited and placed into His kingdom, we have not received all there is in the Kingdom. In fact, we are in a process of regularly receiving more of the Kingdom until that final day when He returns and His kingdom will be fully manifest. The writer of Hebrews tells us we are in the process of receiving a kingdom.

> *"Wherefore we receiving a kingdom which cannot be moved, let us have grace, whereby we may serve God acceptably with reverence and godly fear: (Hebrews 12:28)*

For our current discussion, the focus of this verse is on the word *"receiving"* and its application for us today. The original Greek used here is *paralambano* and means, *"to take with oneself, to join to oneself, to receive something transmitted"* (Thayer's). Now to me, the exciting point of this word is the fact it is a verb in the present active mood: meaning, **we are presently and actively involved in receiving the Kingdom.**

The Kingdom we are receiving is one that cannot be shaken. Why? Simply put, it is His plan! It has been His intent or plan to establish His manifested dominion or reign since creation and Adam. The Kingdom IS His plan!

Now I am not claiming that the fullness of the Kingdom is here, but I am saying that at our new birth, we are placed into His kingdom spiritually. We now become part of the kingdom of priests to minister and demonstrate who He is to this world. We are his representatives or ambassadors, to show this world what it will be like to live under his reign. Eventually, at His coming, he will literally establish His kingdom on earth and sit on the throne of David. Until then, we are to live in Kingdom authority, demonstrating the greatness of our King.

In subsequent chapters we will unpack in greater detail the significance of what it means to be sent as His representatives to demonstrate His kingdom, thereby revealing His glory. For now, suffice it to say that He is actively calling us into a specific place, His Kingdom for a purpose.

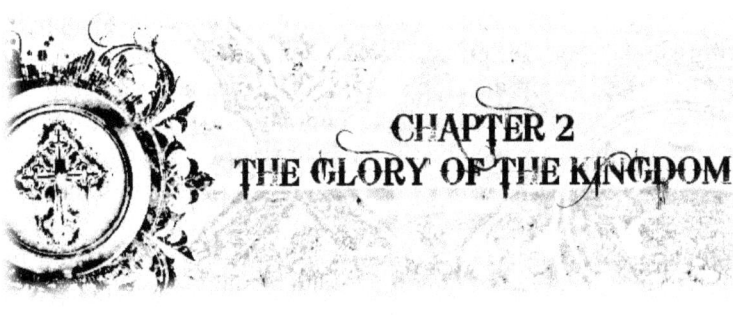

CHAPTER 2
THE GLORY OF THE KINGDOM

Strong lives are motivated by dynamic purposes
~ Kenneth Hildebrand

Purpose Determines Structure

The definition of purpose is: "what something is used for" "an anticipated outcome that is intended or that guides your planned actions" (WordNet 2.0).

The purpose of an object is revealed in how it is created. This purpose determines what it will be used for and the specific actions that will be performed. The structure of a boat was developed because its purpose was to float. The airplane's structure was designed to avail itself of the laws of aerodynamics resulting in the action of flying. While each is an effective and valuable mode of transportation, the plane and boat cannot be switched and expected to produce the same results. Each was designed to take advantage of different principles and function in specific environments.

NASCAR has grown to become the second most popular professional sport in terms of television ratings inside the U.S., ranking behind only the National Football League.[1] Currently the style of cars used is based on four door American made cars. The current eligible cars include the Ford Fusion, Dodge Charger and Chevy Monte Carlo.[2] While these cars have a passing resemblance to what you and I would find on the street, their purpose has resulted in them being built differently. An average engine for NASCAR can be 358 cubic inch V8 with 720 horsepower compared to one of our average car's 3.1L V6 160 horsepower. NASCAR's can achieve speeds over 200mph, while our average cars, even if it was legal, are far from obtaining these speeds. Why the difference? It is in their purpose. The NASCAR is designed for high speeds, with short duration of use, while the average car is supposed to be built for a longer life span and for slower speeds on city streets. While they both are cars, the difference is in their purpose, which is translated into how they are designed, built and maintained.

God Creates With A Purpose

Since the purpose of something is revealed in its creation process, this leads us to ask the question: Why create the earth? Why the biblical creation process?

In an examination of the creation process of Genesis chapter one, God is seen at work designing His creation to fulfill a specific purpose. He spoke light into existence because there was darkness. He divided the waters that were under the firmament from those that were above and he separated the water from the dry land because the earth was without form and void. This existing condition of the earth was not useful for His purpose, so He created what was necessary to fulfill His plans. Now that there was an atmosphere with oxygen and dry land for the grass and herbs to grow, animal life could be created. Because the earth had been created and formed according to a purpose, it was able to function as it was designed--to support life. Subsequently, there were the land animals, the fowl of the air and the creatures of the sea. All were created to fulfill a purpose of God's plan.

We see in the creation process that God created a world of light and beauty that now will sustain life. To this world of chaos and darkness, He spoke and it was so. This is all fine and good but why? Lets read on.

God is a god of order and purpose, the very nature of the creation process demonstrates this. To this well ordered ecosystem of life, called earth, God intended to add more. The following texts give us a glimpse to his purpose for the earth.

> *"But as truly as I live, all the earth shall be filled with the glory of the LORD." (Numbers 14:21)*

> *"And one cried unto another, and said, Holy, holy, holy, is the LORD of hosts: the whole earth is full of his glory." (Isaiah 6:3)*

> *"For the earth shall be filled with the knowledge of the glory of the LORD, as the waters cover the sea." (Habakkuk 2:14)*

God's plan was for the earth to be filled with His glory. Since the idea of His glory is significant to God, it would behoove us to take a closer look at what the *"glory of God"* actually is.

The Glory Of God

The term *"glory"* in association with God is mentioned frequently in the Old and New Testaments. In most instances you will find it associated with some type of manifestation of God's presence. Such things as lights, clouds, fire or some other observable phenomenon captured the attention of those present.

Biblical resources further support the idea of a recognizable manifestation associated with God's glory. According to the ISBE, the general usage of glory is the emphasis on, *"some external physical characteristic which attracts the attention, and makes the object described by the word significant or prominent."* It further states, *"The reference is most frequently, ... to the external manifestations."*

The most common OT word used for glory in reference to God is *kabhodh* and has as its core meaning, *"to be heavy, weighty"* (NAS Exhaustive Concordance). Again, the ISBE tells us *"weight, heaviness and hence in its primary uses it conveys the idea of some external, physical manifestation of dignity, preeminence or majesty...Most important of all, it describes the form in which Jehovah (Yahweh) reveals Himself or is the sign and manifestation of His presence."* Thus, *kabhodh*, used in reference to God's glory is used in reference to a physical manifestation.

Other resources agree that glory is used in regards to a physical manifestation of God's presence.

- *"The OT refers to God's glory (kabod), His visible presence..."* (Holman's)
- *"In the OT Yahweh's glory is his visible and active presence in the creation"* (Dictionary of Paul And His Letters)
- *"....glory is often associated with the phenomenon of light or fire, sometimes of such overwhelming brilliance and unendurable intensity that it is shrouded in a cloud"* (Dictionary of Paul And His Letters)

There are numerous scriptural examples demonstrating this idea. In Exodus 16:1-10, while God is promising bread in the wilderness, it states, *"the glory of the LORD **appeared** in the cloud"* (emphasis added). At Mt Sinai in Exodus 24:16-17, it tells us the glory of the Lord rested in a cloud over the mountain and the *"**sight** of the glory of the LORD was like devouring fire"* (emphasis added). At the dedication of the tabernacle, we are told in Exodus 40:34-35 that the glory of the Lord, in a cloud form, covered the tabernacle.

Thus, we find throughout the Old Testament, when the glory of the Lord was present there was a physical and visible manifestation. This resulted in the people recognizing they were in the presence of God.

In the New Testament, the most common translated Greek word for glory is *doxa*. The understanding of which, *"presupposes the specialized theological background of the OT"* (Dictionary of Jesus and the Gospels). Therefore, just as in the Old Testament, its context is seen as a physical manifestation of the presence of God.

Dr. Spiro Zodhiates elaborates on *doxa*, stating it is to *"recognize a person or thing for what it is...thus doxa can mean appearance."* He further elaborates: *"it basically refers to the recognition belonging to a person."* Romans 3:23 *"speaks of coming short of or lacking the glory of God, meaning man is not what God intended him to be. He lacks God's image and character." "Doxa may denote appearance, form,.. that appearance of a person or thing which catches the eye or attracts attention, commanding recognition."*[5] Thus we see, even in the New Testament, glory refers to a physical manifestation that brings about recognition.

So let me give us a working definition of glory, it is: **An appearance or form that attracts attention, and causes recognition.** Which, in our context, is the recognition of God.

So we now see that God created the earth to fill it with His form or appearance to attract attention and bring recognition of Himself. How did he plan to do that? Through mankind.

Mankind's Purpose

In the creation process, we are told that Adam (mankind) was to be his crowning work. We now see the reason for the specifics of the creation process and their life sustaining abilities.

> "And God said, Let us make man in our image, after our likeness:" (Genesis 1:26)

> "What is man, that thou art mindful of him? and the son of man, that thou visitest him? For thou hast made him a little lower than the angels, and hast crowned him with glory and honour. Thou madest him to have dominion over the works of thy hands; thou hast put all things under his feet:" (Psalms 8:4-6)

Psalms Eight speaks of God's original plan for the creation of man. Adam was to be the crowning glory of God's creative process. The original place of man was one of glory, honor and dominion. God created a world with an entire ecosystem to support life for one purpose: that He might use Adam, or mankind, to fill the earth with His image, dominion, glory and honor.

> "And God said, Let us make man in our image, after our likeness: and let them have dominion over the fish of the sea, and over the fowl of the air, and over the cattle, and over all the earth, and over every creeping thing that creepeth upon the earth. So God created man in his own image, in the image of God created he him; male and female created he them. And God blessed them, and God said unto them, Be fruitful, and multiply, and replenish the earth, and subdue it: and have dominion over the fish of the sea, and over the fowl of the air, and over every living thing that moveth upon the earth." (Genesis 1:26-28)

Man was created in the image of God, given dominion, told to subdue creation and to replenish the earth. As the image of God he was crowned with glory and honor and it was God's intent to fill the earth with His glory – or his image, through man. Mankind, via Adam, was created to be the glory of God: that form or appearance that would bring recognition of God.

Like Produces Like

God was very detailed in the creation process, making sure that each aspect of the process was completed to fulfill its purpose. The creation of the dry land had an ultimate purpose; it was to bring forth the life forms suited for dry ground. Genesis 1:12 tells us that the Lord commanded the earth to bring forth grass herbs and fruit bearing trees that would reproduce after their kind. Further in verse 24, the earth is commanded to bring forth the animal life that would reproduce after itself and dwell on the earth. This same process was commanded of the waters in verse 20. The idea presented here is that the purpose of creating earth and seas was to produce life that was suited for its respective environment. This individual life that was created was instructed to reproduce after its kind, living in the environment from which it was created.

In all the process of creation, nothing compared to the formation of man. No other part of creation was to carry such importance in His purpose as was mankind. Unlike the rest of creation, man was not spoken into existence, but was formed by the hand of God personally. The creation of man was different because his purpose was different. He was patterned after God Himself. The nature and being of God was his specifications and his life came from the breath of God. His purpose would be to act as God's representative to creation. Therefore, Adam's creation included all that was necessary to express the image of God.

Because of Adam's purpose, the next logical step was for God to give man dominion and authority to accomplish His purpose.

And God said, Let us make man in our image, after our likeness: and let them have dominion ...28 And

> *God blessed them, and God said unto them, Be fruitful, and multiply, and replenish the earth, and subdue it: and have dominion over the fish of the sea, and over the fowl of the air, and over every living thing that moveth upon the earth. (Genesis 1:26-28)*

God gave Adam dominion, which is the right to rule. In other words, he was given authority to rule over what God had created. According to Nelson's Illustrated Bible Dictionary, authority is: *"The power or right to do something, particularly to give orders and see that they are followed. The word authority as used in the Bible usually means a person's right to do certain things because of the position or office he holds. This word emphasizes the legality and right, more than the physical strength, needed to do something."* Adam was given the authority to rule God's creation.

There are some key principles to understanding and operating effectively in Kingdom authority. First, the source of authority comes from outside the one operating in authority. Second, authority has a specific area or place to operate. Third, there is usually a specific mission or purpose for the use of authority. Finally, it requires obedience and complete follow-through for authority to be effective. These concepts will be elaborated on in subsequent chapters, but we can see them demonstrated in Adam. He was placed in the garden with instructions to subdue it and have dominion. This authority was exercised when the Lord brought the beasts of the field and the fowls of the air to him to see what he would call them.

Summary

As God's representative, mankind's commission was to be fruitful, multiply and replenish the earth. Specifically, he was to replenish it with the image of God, having dominion or authority over creation. God gave Adam the legal right to command or speak to creation, therefore He expected obedience.

The purpose for Kingdom authority is to continue the purpose God has for mankind, which is to fill the earth with His image. To accomplish this He has given to the church, the born again believers, His authority to conduct His business. Unfortunately, we see that once again mankind has failed to accomplish this purpose. In the next chapter we will discuss the greatest hindrance we have to operating in the authority God has given to us.

1. http://en.wikipedia.org/wiki/NASCAR; Wikipedia, the free encyclopedia
2. (About Inc.)
3. Lexical Aids to the New Testament, Spiro Zodhiates, TH.D, The Hebrew- Greek Keynote Study Bible, 1984 & 1991, AMG International, Inc

CHAPTER 3
IN HIS IMAGE

Representative: One that serves as a delegate or agent for another. ~ *American Heritage Dictionary*

And God said, Let us make man in our image, after our likeness: and let them have dominion...
(Genesis 1:26)

Genesis 1:26 gives wonderful insight into God's purpose for mankind. Adam was created in the image and likeness of God. At a casual glance this may seem like a simple statement, but it has a depth of truth that is foundational to our purpose of living in Kingdom authority.

When God chose to make Adam, he stated two forms of expression that pertained to Adam, image and likeness. Examining these individually, we see further depth to Adam's and thus mankind's purpose.

Image

The word used in this text for *"image"* is *tselem* and means *"statue; copy"* (Vine's). Many of its usages are in the sense of a replica of something. The following is a common scenario illustrating an image and its significance.

You're at the store, ready to check out with your credit or debit card and the clerk asks you, "Can I see some ID please?" So what do you do? You reach for your driver's license. Ok, so what is so different about this 2x3 piece of plastic, that it would ease the mind of the suspicious (or bored) clerk? Well duh! It has your picture on it. So what?

Once we have given them the driver's license, the clerk looks at the picture, and then looks up at you, then back at the picture. Why? They are comparing you to the image on the card. **It is this image that is used to confirm your identity.** Please note - the image is not you, it is a replica or copy of you, but it causes others to recognize you.

So what is an image? *"a representation of a person or thing"* (Dictionary.com). An image is not the actual thing or person, but it is something that is used for identification.

From this perspective, we can grasp that as God's image, Adam was His chosen method to reveal Himself to creation. It was through Adam an invisible God made himself not only visible, but recognizable.

Likeness

Now lets turn our attention to the word likeness. The original word used here is *demut* and has as a basic meaning: *"likeness; shape; figure; form; pattern"* (Vine's). The idea of pattern is the sense of *"the specification from which an actual item is made"* (Vine's). A pattern is used to make sure the product being made functions according to the specifications. Blueprints are a pattern for a house: the layout of the electrical, plumbing, walls and other specifications are on the patterns so when finished the house will be livable or function correctly.

We also find that the word *"likeness"* actually amplifies the meaning of *"image"* meaning. *"Man ...is not simply representative but representational. Man is the visible, corporeal representative of the invisible, bodiless God"* (TWOT). The idea conveyed here is a functional one. It is Adam acting for God, thus demonstrating by those actions the nature and identity of God.

To summarize, *likeness* refers to the representational aspect of God's image. As God's likeness, Adam was to ACT as God's representative thereby revealing the nature and characteristics of God. Adam's representational purpose was manifest when he obeyed God's command, demonstrating his dominion by naming the animals.

As God's image and likeness, Adam was to reveal to all of creation what God was like: his purpose was to make God tangible or real, ruling as God's representative. Through Adam, God's nature and character would be expressed. Thus we have God's glory revealed: a form or appearance, attracting attention resulting in the recognition of who God was. If he had been obedient, as he and Eve had offspring, eventually the earth would have been filled with the image or glory of God. This was God's plan for Adam or mankind and it still his plan regarding the Kingdom.

From this point on, we see the Good News (gospel) being worked out: not just to redeem man, but also to restore him back to his original purpose. A study of the scriptures reveals a focused part of the Good News is a restoration back to the image and representation of God. This is seen first in the purpose of Jesus, then applied to the born again believer.

The Significance Of Adam's Sin

Unfortunately, we all understand Adam disobeyed and it resulted in more than their expulsion from the garden. Because of his sin, Adam was no longer in the image and likeness of God and he lost the privilege to be God's representative to creation. Not only was Adam affected, but also his sin and its consequences were transferred to all mankind. Paul tells us in Romans 5:12 *"When Adam sinned, sin entered the world. Adam's sin brought death, so death spread to everyone, for everyone sinned." (NLT)*

Again, Paul in writing to the church at Rome summarizes the significance of Adams disobedience. *"For all have sinned, and come short of the glory of God" (Romans 3:23).* Viewing this text from the context of Adam and mankind's purpose reveals the catastrophic effects of Adam's actions and gives us insight into the purpose and power of the Gospel.

The common word in the New Testament used for sin or sinned is *hamartano* and its basic meaning is, *"to miss the mark"* (Strong's). The idea that comes to mind is to miss a target, goal or some objective. So what could this be? The verse clearly tells us: it is *"the glory of God."* Using the previous definition of glory, it can be stated we have all *"missed the mark and come short of the form or appearance that attracts attention, bringing recognition of God!"* Exactly what Adam and mankind were supposed to do! Unfortunately, we now also are unable because we too miss the mark.

Jesus Is About Restoration

Warning! ~ *The following paragraphs could be challenging to a traditionalists mindset of Jesus' purpose and the Gospel. Before you judge, please take some time to pray and study out the texts. Take what I say at face value, do not read anything into my words.*

It is my opinion, based on observation and study, that modern North American Christianity focuses on a self-centered bless me gospel. In most cases, the gospel and the word of God are viewed in a context of how it will impact my life. The born again experience is seen as an avoidance of hell, or securing a ticket to a heavenly paradise. The word of God is searched like a self-help manual looking for that right formula to fix the current dilemma.

We even go as far as to base our commitment to a local assembly on how it benefits my family's or my perceived needs. Our faithfulness, involvement and giving are predicated on what we get out of it. Thus, church leadership has resorted to a consumerist buffet of glitzy programs designed to appeal to our self-centeredness.

Now, I am not saying the leadership of these churches are insincere and lacking a desire to reach people. Unfortunately, they are bogged down in a quagmire of man's religious system (see chapter 10 on tradition). Neither am I saying it is wrong to have good programs: I'm speaking of the focus, motive, and intent or whatever term you want to use of why the average believer is "living for God."

I believe the root issue of our self-centered religious lifestyle is due to a faulty context of Gospel presentation. It seems for much of Christianity, the Gospel consists of the fall of man (sin) and his redemption. Now what I mean is, the focus is on man, even though the redemption was by Jesus, **we focus on it's effect on man, instead of its relationship to the big plan of God.** Hang on! Stay with me here as I elaborate.

Remember in chapter one we discussed Jesus' first message? It **was not** repent and get saved or go to heaven. But it **was** repent, because the Kingdom was near. I submit, we should view the Gospel or good news in a Kingdom context, not in a self-context.

Accurately, it can be said that the good news consists of four parts: Creation, Fall (sin), Redemption and Restoration. Instead of our focus being on the fall and redemption, we should view the Gospel with God's original purpose for man and creation. **The end result of the Gospel is restoration back to God's original plan of image and dominion.** If this is our context, we will view the fall and redemption with greater significance.

Now, with this in mind, lets view Jesus' act of redemption and its greater significance ~ restoration.

Regarding the restoration aspect of the Gospel, Jesus came to restore what Adam lost. To the church at Corinth, Paul wrote: *"The first man Adam became a living being. The last Adam became a life-giving spirit" (1 Corinthians 15:45).* In this statement, he is linking Jesus to Adam. The term *"last"* means *"extreme, last in time or in place"* (Thayer's), so Jesus came as the last in time or place, or the final Adam. What seems to be the implied importance here is the direct linking of Jesus to Adam.

The Keil & Delitzch Commentary on the Old Testament adds further confirmation of this in the following quote: *"This spiritual seed culminated in Christ, in whom the Adamitic family terminated, henceforward to be renewed by Christ as the second Adam,* **and restored by Him to its original exaltation and likeness to God**" (emphasis added). So Jesus came to restore what Adam lost: God's manifest image on this earth.

Jesus Christ, as the last Adam, came as the visible image of an invisible God. Speaking of Jesus, Paul tells us he is *"the image of God" (2 Corinthians 4:4)* and the *"image of the invisible God" (Colossians 1:15).* The writer of Hebrews makes it a little more personal stating that Jesus is *"the radiance of God's glory and the exact representation of his being" (Hebrews 1:3 NIV).* With our understanding of the meaning of glory and the above verses, it is no wonder that Jesus stated, *"he that hath seen me hath seen the Father" (John 14:9).* Jesus restored what Adam lost – the image of God on the earth.

Just like Adam, Jesus was more than an image of God; he was representational of the invisible God. Jesus stated that *"I have manifested thy name unto the men which thou gavest me out of the world" (John 17:6).* The word translated *"manifested"* is a verb that means, *"to make visible, clear, manifest"* (Vine's). Thayer's says it is making visible or known *"what has been hidden or unknown, whether by words, **or deeds**"* (emphasis added). Jesus came making an invisible God more than visible; he came to make him knowable by demonstration.

Jesus came to restore what Adam was created to be - the image and representation of God on earth. The Good News or Gospel is about Jesus' death, burial and resurrection, **resulting** in restoration of the original purpose and authority lost by Adam.

Just as the scripture shows us that the first and last Adams were each to be a representational image of an invisible God, so we who are born again are to be representational. Paul tells us *"as we have borne the image of the man of dust, we shall also bear the image of the heavenly Man" (1 Corinthians 15:49 NKJV).* Just as we have born the image of our fallen nature, we are to bear the image of a new Heavenly man, Jesus.

Regarding this new man, we are told it is after the knowledge of the one that created us. Colossians 3:10 states that we *"have put on the new man, which is renewed in knowledge after **the image of him that created him**"* (emphasis added). In this text, *"in"* is eis, which is *"into, indicating the point reached or entered"* (Strong's). *"Knowledge"* is epignosis, which means *"recognition, full discernment"* (Strong's). So this verse could be read as follows:

> *And have put on the new man, which is renewed into, indicating the point reached or entered, full discernment after the representation and manifestation of him that created him*

In Ephesians 2:24, we are instructed to *"put on the new man;"* but what type of new man? One that is *"after God."* But what does this really mean? Two other translations reveal to us it is the image and likeness of God.

> *"and to clothe yourselves with the new nature, which was created **according to God's image** in righteousness and true holiness"(ISV emphasis added)*

> *"created **after the likeness of God** in true righteousness and holiness" (ESV emphasis added)*

This new nature we are to put on or clothe ourselves with is created after the image and likeness of God.

Just as the scripture shows us that the first and last Adams were each to be a representational image of an invisible God, so **we who are born again are to be representational because:**

- We are bearing the image of the heavenly
- We are renewed after the image of the one that created us
- We are conformed to the image of Jesus

As His body, the church is to manifest Jesus Christ to this dark and confused world.

> *"So all of us who have had that veil removed can see and reflect the glory of the Lord. And the Lord--who is the Spirit--makes us more and more like him as we are changed into his glorious image" (2 Corinthians 3:18 NLT)*

The Gospel Context

For the Son of man is come to seek and to save that which was lost. (Luke 19:10)

Many are familiar with this text: however, it is common to hear this text miss quoted and applied. Most I believe, will say that Jesus came to save those that were lost, implying it is people that he came for. Now I am not denying He is concerned about people, but I believe there is a greater meaning here that goes beyond the salvation message.

Looking at the basic meanings of the original language gives us significant insight to this text. The word *"save"* is from the Greek *sozo* and can mean, *"whole, heal or preserve"* (Vine's). *"That which was lost"* is one word in the original, and means, *"to destroy, abolish, put an end to or ruin"* (Thayer's). So Jesus came to seek and heal or make whole what had been destroyed, abolished or ruined. What had been destroyed? It was God's representational image on the earth!

The context of the good news or Gospel is the restoration of God's kingdom plan. It is the restoration of His representational image and dominion on the earth. We have been born again to a new nature, one that includes His representational image.

As His body, the church is to manifest Jesus Christ to this dark and confused world. We have been authorized to conduct business as representatives of the Kingdom of Jesus Christ. We are to walk in His delegated authority as we demonstrate to this world what His kingdom will be like. By manifestation and representation, we reveal to this world there is something better. We reveal to them that there is a King and He is coming with His kingdom and His name is Jesus!

> *As you sent me into the world, I am sending them into the world. (John 17:18 NLT)*

The next chapter will elaborate on the authority we have been given and what it means to really be apostolic.

CHAPTER 4
THE REAL APOSTOLICS

A church with apostolic foundations is that body of people whose central impulse and principle of life, being and service is one thing only, namely, a radical and total jealousy for the glory of God. ~ Art Katz

Many churches today refer to themselves as apostolic. This is based on a number of different reasons. One is a belief that there is a continuation of apostolic succession, beginning with Peter and subsequently passed on to appropriate leaders. Others claim to be apostolic because their teachings are similar to the doctrines taught by the original twelve apostles. Still, there are others who have a church organizational structure that has developed a hierarchy of individuals with one at the top declaring themselves to be an apostle. The underlying fundamental belief of this structure is that there should be an authority present in the church that is referred to as apostolic authority. Unfortunately, for most, the authority that is present is only structural, with limited spiritual confirmation by signs and wonders. These applications of what is thought to be an apostolic model are a result of the misunderstanding of what apostolic authority is and its appropriate application to ministry.

Obviously, I have an opinion regarding what it means to be apostolic. In using this terminology, I believe we are speaking of the authority that Jesus first demonstrated which was then passed on to the apostles and the first century church. This authority was evidenced by powerful messages that were confirmed by miraculous signs and wonders. Currently there are some groups whose focus is on the manifestation of authority and the miraculous outcome. However, there appears to be a lack of understanding of the source, means of transmission and biblical usage of apostolic and it's application to Kingdom authority.

To bring some clarification, we must look at the biblical basis of the terminology apostolic and authority. An examination of the biblical definitions of the words power, authority and apostolic will assist us in establishing a firm foundation for us to build upon.

Power

In the New Testament we see two words that are translated as power, they are *dunamis* and *exousia*. It is significant to understand the meaning of each and its application to Kingdom authority.

- *Dunamis* means: *"strength, ability or power. It refers to an inherent power, a power residing in a thing by virtue of its nature."* (Thayer's)

- *Exousia*, on the other hand: *"denotes a freedom of action or right to act."* (Vine's)

- *Authority*, according to Nelsons Illustrated Bible dictionary is*: "the power or right to do something, particularly to give orders and see that they are followed. It means a persons right to do certain things, It emphasizes the legality and right more than physical strength."*

Putting this in perspective, *dunamis* or power, is the strength or ability to do something while *exousia* or authority, is the legal right to use the *dunamis* of another and expect results. This difference between power and authority is imperative to our understanding if we desire to minister and live in Kingdom authority. *Dunamis* or power is something inherent (abiding within) by virtue or nature of an individual. *Exousia* or authority is from an external source, it is the legal right to use another's, i.e. Jesus Christ's, *dunamis*.

A good illustration can be seen in a common scenario exhibited on our highways. A particular driver may be stopped for speeding by a five foot two, one hundred and ten pound police officer. This driver is taller, heavier and stronger and could "take them." However, the driver is respectful and holds his peace, because he is aware of who this officer represents. In examining this illustration it is apparent that the driver of the car may have a certain amount of power or *dunamis* that is greater than the power or *dunamis* of the police officer. However, the officer has more *exousia* or authority. They have the legal right to use the power or *dunamis* of the government they are representing, and this power is greater than that of the driver.

The application of this to Kingdom authority is this: authority is not based on our ability or strength; it is based on using the strength or ability of another, specifically Jesus Christ. His power is to be used in the manner that He authorizes or prescribes. This is a liberating truth to comprehend: the power to operate in Kingdom authority does not originate within me. The source of this miraculous ability is from Jesus Christ himself.

Apostolic

The next term to grasp in understanding Kingdom authority is the word apostolic. This word is not found in scripture, but it is an adjective used to describe the type of authority that is desired. This term is used in reference to the type of ministry manifest by the apostles in the Book of Acts. An exploration of the scriptural words used in association with the apostles will give us great insight into their ability to operate with such authority. Two words that are significant are apostle and sent. To more fully understand, we need to explore the words used in relationship to the apostles. An understanding of these will give us insight into how the apostles could be used of the Lord in the miraculous manner that we see.

The main word translated apostle is *apostolos*. The following sources give a detailed definition of the meaning and function of an apostle:

- Vine's says it is *"one sent forth."*
- Thayer's says it is *"a delegate, messenger or one sent forth with orders."*
- Holman Bible Dictionary says it is *"a person sent to accomplish a mission. An apostle represents the one sending and has authority to represent the sender in business, political or educational situations."*
- The International Standard Bible Encyclopedia says *"there is a difference between a messenger (aggelos) and an apostolos. The apostolos was more than a messenger, they were a delegate or representative of the one who sent them."*
- The Dictionary of Jesus and the Gospels states, *"the apstelleo is used to denote the sending of a person with a commission."* A commission is an authorization to act for, in behalf of or in place of another.

Included in the definitions above, is the concept of being sent or a sending. In regard to this, the Greek word for send or sent is *apostelloo* and means *"properly, to send off, send away"* (Thayer's). It includes the idea of sending for a *"service, or with a commission"* (Vine's). In essence, it is sending someone to act as another's representative.

One of the challenges we have grasping biblical truths is that we tend to view everything from a biblical context. Many times we fail to grasp that the chosen words were commonly used in the daily life of that culture. I think this usage was intentional: either to bring the common meaning to a spiritual concept or to challenge the cultural context. The former is what I believe happened with the word *apostelloe*.

It was common in the New Testament times for individuals to send someone as a commissioned representative. This could be as simple as delivering a message, or something quite significant such as a military action. The following lists of texts give us non-spiritual examples of someone being *apostelleo*. In each of the following examples the emphasized words are from the Greek *apostelleo*.

- Herod **"sent forth"** and slew the children (Matthew 2:16)
- While Jesus was at Gennesaret, they **"sent out"** for the diseased (Matthew 14:35)
- The Pharisees **"sent out"** their disciples to "entangle him in his words" (Matthew 22:15)
- Pilate's wife **"sent"** to him advising to have nothing to do with Jesus (Matthew 27:19)
- John **"sent"** his disciples to Jesus (Luke 7:20)
- Jesus **"sent"** out the seventy (Luke 10:1)
- Chief priests and scribes **"sent"** spies to trap Jesus (Luke 20:20)
- Herod **"sent"** forth and laid hold of John (Mark 6:17)
- Herod **"sent"** the executioner and beheaded John (Mark 6:27)
- Angel Gabriel **"sent"** to Mary (Luke 1:26)

These individuals were all *apostelloe* – or sent. They were commissioned to act as the representatives of the one who sent them. This then, makes them *apostolos* (apostles) or apostolic.

Apostles are those who are special delegates, authorized or commissioned with a specific purpose and sent to represent or carry out transactions for the one authorizing and sending. They are authorized to use the *dunamis* or power of the one who sent them. What delineates the importance here is **who is doing the sending**. The greater the power of the one sending, the greater the authority of the one sent.

Thayer's elaborates further on *apostelloe* and tells us there are four components to this sending:

- First, they are ordered to go.
- Secondly, they are sent with a commission or something intended for another.
- Thirdly, the place of their sending is specific.
- Fourth, the completion or manifestation of the duty is proof of the sending.

These four components in the definition of *apostelloo* are evident in the delegation of authority Jesus Christ gives to believers. First, it is Jesus Christ who calls us to go. Secondly, we are sent with specific orders or purpose to achieve. Thirdly, the Lord specifies the area we are sent to. And fourthly, as we endeavor to be obedient and perform the task instructed, He confirms our words with the miraculous demonstration of His power. Therefore, to be *apostolos*, or an apostle, is to be sent as a special delegate or envoy, authorized to represent and carry out transactions for the one that is authorizing and sending. Those that are *apostolos* do not use their own *dunamis* or power. They are authorized or empowered to use the *dunamis* or power of the one sending them.

Therefore, living in Kingdom authority rests on the principle of being apostolic or authorized and sent to use the power of the One who has sent us, conducting business for Him. Living in Kingdom authority is not based on the individual's inherent power or ability, therefore anyone can be sent. The weakest, the uneducated, those who are not part of the "in" crowd can all be sent with authority. Since it is delegated authority, the responsibility to produce is not with the one being sent. The only responsibility for the correct usage of Kingdom authority is a submission to His will, using His power for His purpose.

Jesus Is our Example.

And are built upon the foundation of the apostles and prophets, Jesus Christ himself being the chief corner stone; (Ephesians 2:20)

Wherefore, holy brethren, partakers of the heavenly calling, consider the Apostle and High Priest of our profession, Christ Jesus; Who was faithful to him that appointed him, as also Moses was faithful in all his house. (Hebrews 3:1-2)

We are to build our understanding of Kingdom authority on the apostles and prophets, anchoring ourselves into Jesus Christ as the cornerstone. Hebrews tells us that Jesus is the Apostle and High Priest of our profession. If Jesus is the Apostle and we are to be anchored to Him, it is to Him we must look for our example of Kingdom authority.

Jesus himself speaks of being sent. Hebrews says that as the Apostle, He *"was faithful to him that appointed him" (Hebrews 3:1)*. Thayer's defines faithful as: *"one who shows themselves faithful in the transaction of business, the execution of commands or the discharge of official duties."* Jesus was faithful to carry out the purpose of the one who sent Him. This faithfulness was evidenced in His statement in the Gospel of John: *"And this is life eternal, that they might know thee the only true God, and Jesus Christ, whom thou hast sent. I have glorified thee on the earth: I have finished the work which thou gavest me to do" (John 17:3-4)*.

As the Apostle, Jesus was sent with a specific commission, to a specific people and place and His coming and ministry revealed the purpose of his sending. Throughout His ministry, we find Him expressing often that the words He spoke and the works He performed were not His. In the following list of scriptures, Jesus emphatically states that He was doing the will of the one who sent Him.

> *Then answered Jesus and said unto them, Verily, verily, I say unto you, The Son can do nothing of himself, but what he seeth the Father do: for what things soever he doeth, these also doeth the Son likewise. (John 5:19)*

> *For I came down from heaven, not to do mine own will, but the will of him that sent me. (John 6:38)*

> *Jesus answered them, and said, My doctrine is not mine, but his that sent me. (John 7:16)*

> *Then said Jesus unto them, When ye have lifted up the Son of man, then shall ye know that I am he, and that I do nothing of myself; but as my Father hath taught me, I speak these things. (John 8:28)*

> *For I have not spoken of myself; but the Father which sent me, he gave me a commandment, what I should say, and what I should speak. (John 12:49)*

> *And I know that his commandment is life everlasting: whatsoever I speak therefore, even as the Father said unto me, so I speak. (John 12:50)*

> *For I have given unto them the words which thou gavest me; and they have received them, and have known surely that I came out from thee, and they have believed that thou didst send me. (John 17:8)*

Believest thou not that I am in the Father, and the Father in me? the words that I speak unto you I speak not of myself: but the Father that dwelleth in me, he doeth the works. (John 14:10)

Therefore, with Jesus Christ as our example, we are sent forth to operate in Kingdom authority just as He was sent. We are to faithfully perform the will of the one who sends us, speaking the words and conducting the business as we have been instructed. Only then will we be able to expect His power to be revealed.

Empowered

And, behold, I send the promise of my Father upon you: but tarry ye in the city of Jerusalem, until ye be endued with power from on high. (Luke 24:49)

When we are baptized with the Holy Ghost, we are endued with a power that is not of this world. In the above text, The Amplified Bible says *"until ye are clothed with power from on high."* In *Acts 1:8,* Jesus promised His disciples; *"ye shall receive power, after that the Holy Ghost is come upon you:"* In both these text, power is the *dunamis* we defined earlier, the inherent ability to perform the miraculous. With the indwelling of His Spirit, we are clothed with a power that does not come from us, but originates in the spirit realm.

Paul, writing to Timothy states: *"And I thank Christ Jesus our Lord, who hath enabled me, for that he counted me faithful, putting me into the ministry;" (1 Timothy 1:12).* This enabling is from the Greek *endunamoo,* which means: *"to empower"* (Strong's). To the church at Ephesus, Paul instructed to: *"be strong in the Lord, and the power of his might" (Ephesians 6:10).* To be strong is also the Greek *endunamoo, "to be empowered in the Lord and the power of his might."* As a born again believer, we are not to operate in our own ability, but we are to be clothed and empowered with the Lord's power. It is this power that gives us the ability to operate in Kingdom authority. We should then, by faith use His power that we have been clothed and empowered with.

We Are Sent

"As thou hast sent me into the world, even so have I also sent them into the world". (John 17:18)

"... as my Father hath sent me, even so send I you." (John 20:21)

As the Apostle, Jesus understood what it meant to be sent. In the texts above, Jesus is sending or transferring the authorization to us, His disciples. Jesus states that as He has been sent into the world, He has sent us into the world. One of the keys to operating in Kingdom authority is an understanding of who sends us.

Jesus stated in *Matthew 28:18 "All power is given unto me in heaven and in earth."* The Amplified Bible says: *"All authority (all power of rule)"* was given to Him. He followed up this statement in the next verse with a commissioning of His disciples. *"Go ye therefore, and make disciples of all the nations, baptizing them into the name of the Father and of the Son and of the Holy Spirit:" (ASV Matthew 28:19)*. Jesus was applying the principle of apostolic sending. In Acts 1:8 after proclaiming *"ye shall receive power,"* the next point was how to use that power: *"ye shall be my witnesses."* The purpose of receiving His Spirit and its empowering was that we would be sent forth to proclaim Him, using the authority to manifest Him to a lost world.

Summary

We have been empowered, authorized and sent as special messengers to conduct business in His name. What is that business? We are to make disciples. We are sent and authorized to use divine power. We have been endued with power from outside of us, which is now in us, but not of us. This power in us goes with us where we are sent, revealing itself as we exercise the authority, right, and privilege we have been given.

CHAPTER 5
YOUR PLACE OF AUTHORITY

Authority is not a quality one person "has," in the sense that he has property or physical qualities. Authority refers to an interpersonal relation in which one person looks upon another as somebody superior to him. ~ Erich Fromm

Part of the definition of being sent is that there is a specific place to which we are sent. This implies that someone of a greater authority is designating where I am to operate my authority. To the extent that I am submitted to authority, determines the level of authority I can operate in. Again, using Jesus as our example, we see that He was submitted to the one who sent him. This resulted in His ability to manifest the authority and power of God. His submission was evident by what He said and did. The words that were spoken and the works that were manifest were not His, but of the one who sent Him. The following scriptures substantiate that He was submitted to the will of the Father:

> *For I came down from heaven, not to do mine own will, but the will of him that sent me (John 6:38)*

> *Jesus answered them, and said, My doctrine is not mine, but his that sent me (John 7:16)*
>
> *Then said Jesus unto them, When ye have lifted up the Son of man, then shall ye know that I am he, and that I do nothing of myself; but as my Father hath taught me, I speak these things.(John 8:28)*
>
> *For I have not spoken of myself; but the Father which sent me, he gave me a commandment, what I should say, and what I should speak. (John 12:49)*
>
> *And I know that his commandment is life everlasting: whatsoever I speak therefore, even as the Father said unto me, so I speak. (John 12:50)*
>
> *For I have given unto them the words which thou gavest me; and they have received them, and have known surely that I came out from thee, and they have (John 17:8)*

Jesus Himself said He came down from heaven, not to perform His own will, but the will of the one who sent Him. He further states that His doctrine was actually not His, but it was of the one who sent Him. This is truly apostolic: being in submission to the authority of the one who is sending. As a result of not seeking His own will, we see His ministry was one of the miraculous.

Demonstrating Kingdom authority is based on my submission to being apostolic (sent). This means I must grasp that:

- It is God's idea
- It is God's power
- It is God's mission
- He is the one authorizing me

- AND he expects His results!

Therefore, to be qualified to use Kingdom authority, I must:
- Go where He sends me
- Say what He tells me to say
- Do what He tells me to do

Then I can expect Him to confirm his words with miraculous demonstration. Any other actions on my part could really be considered rebellion.

Sons of Sceva

Failure to be in submission to authority can result in our lack of authority because we cannot be trusted. In Acts 19:13-17 we observe the failure of certain individuals who attempt to operate in Kingdom authority without being themselves submitted to authority. There were seven sons of a man named Sceva who were vagabond Jews. They took upon themselves to call the name of Jesus over those who were filled with evil spirits. They invoked the name of Jesus who Paul preaches. Unfortunately for them, it states that the spirits recognized Jesus and Paul, but questioned who they were. Subsequently, the man who was possessed of the spirit lept on them, prevailed physically, and forced them to flee from the house wounded and naked.

Examining this incident closer we see two potential reasons for their failure. First they were vagabonds. This word has been translated as wander, wanderer or vacillate. They were individuals who did not have a place to settle and were not committed anywhere. They were men looking unto themselves. Secondly we see they were the sons of one Sceva. Holman Bible Dictionary says of Sceva: *"No such Jewish high priest is known from other sources, particularly not one living in Ephesus. The title may be the result of a copyist or a title Sceva took upon himself to impress leaders of other religions in Ephesus."* If this is correct, we see that the father, Sceva, was a man who desired to lift himself up in the eyes of others and was not submitted to authority. This attitude exemplified by Sceva could have been passed on to his sons. The combination of these two attitudes seems to have resulted in sons who wanted authority but were not willing to walk in submission. Subsequently, when they attempted to exercise authority they failed.

For us to walk in the same authority that Jesus did, we must be submitted as He was. In placing ourselves under God's structure of authority we can be assured that He will willingly authorize us to use His power.

A final interesting note in this story is the response of the spirit to these men. It said *"Jesus I know and Paul I know."* In this text, the English word *know* is translated from two different Greek words, each revealing a unique level of knowledge.

Regarding the demons knowledge of Jesus, the Greek word translated for *"know"* is *"ginosko"* and according to Vine's, it means: *"to be taking in knowledge, to come to know, recognize, understand,"* or *"to understand completely."* Further, Vine's states, "*In the NT ginosko frequently indicates a relation between the person "knowing" and the object known; in this respect, what is "known" is of value or importance to the one who knows, and hence the establishment of the relationship."* Obviously, as a fallen angel, the demon would have an intimate knowledge of his creator and His abilities.

When speaking of Paul, the demon used the Greek word *"epistamai"* and has the meaning of *"standing upon, referring to gaining knowledge by prolonged acquaintance, i.e. sustained, personal effort. It expresses what comes from close and familiar acquaintance"* (Helps™ Word Studies). So, it could be said that Paul was attracting the attention of the demon and was developing a reputation in the spirit realm.

Both Jesus and Paul were submitted to authority, Jesus as the Apostle coming to do the will of the one who sent him, and Paul an apostle doing the will of Jesus who sent him. These men were under authority and they were known in the spirit realm.

One of my ministry trips took me to Pakistan where I was privileged to minister these principles at three pastoral leadership conferences. During one of the meetings, a missionary pointed out a Pakistani pastor, Sultan Abbas, and told me his story.

It seems that in a particular city, there was a family whose mother was possessed. They had sought the known Christian ministers to come and cast out the demon. However, each one failed, many leaving mentally or physically shaken up. It was reported that on each occasion the demon would speak out that he was so strong that no one could cast him out.

After one particular failed attempt by a new minister in town, this demon spoke out in a boastful manner: "I am so strong that not even Sultan Abbas can cast me out!" Now this family had not heard of Sultan Abbas and they began inquiring in their city of 35,000 for this individual.

After a two month search they located Sultan Abbas and explained the situation to him; asking if he could come and cast the demon out of their mother. He readily agreed and was taken to her.

The missionary relayed the story that when Sultan Abbas walked into the mother's room, the demon began to rise up and manifest as usual. However, Sultan Abbas immediately took authority in the name of Jesus and commanded the demon to leave. And this time, the demon left! The point of this story: the family did not know Sultan Abbas, but because he walked in submitted authority, the demons knew who he was! He obviously had a reputation in the spirit realm!

Could it be that as we submit ourselves to authority and begin to operate in authority, that even the spirits know who we are?

Knowing Our Place

In the story of the Canaanite woman who came to Jesus begging for her daughter's deliverance, Jesus makes a statement as to the specific place he had been sent. *"...I am not sent but unto the lost sheep of the house of Israel" (Matthew 15:24)*. Once again the word for sent is *apostelloo*; meaning he had been commissioned and sent to a specific place, for a specific purpose. As an Apostle, demonstrating Kingdom authority, Jesus understood that there was a specific area or group of people he was sent to. This was necessary because the words He was given, the works He did, and the commandments He imparted were specifically for the house of Israel. If He were to go where he decided, he would not have been obedient to the one who sent Him, and would not have accomplished the purpose He was sent for. By submitting His ministry to the specific place he was sent, a freedom to operate in authority was produced.

Operating in Kingdom authority requires knowledge of the specific area or arena of ministry we are sent to. Knowing where we are placed and submitting to authority allows a freedom to exercise authority. In Luke 7, we read of a centurion who sent friends to Jesus because of a sick servant. He requested that Jesus should just say the word and his servant would be healed. In his explanation for this request, it is obvious that this centurion understood what it meant to be sent or placed in a specific position of authority. In verse 8 he says *"for I also am a man set under authority, having under me soldiers, and I say unto one, Go, and he goeth; and to another, Come, and he cometh; and to my servant, Do this, and he doeth it."* The centurion knew how authority was ordered or arranged. He knew where he was set in this structure, and he was able to give commands and expect them to be followed. His authority was not of his own ability but was because he was set under authority. Therefore, he had faith to exercise authority within the area he had been set.

Knowledge of the Lord's structure of authority will produce in us a freedom of faith to operate in authority. We are to be under authority if we are to exercise authority. All authority is ordained of God and we can only successfully operate in the level of authority equal to the level of our submission to authority.

God's Structure of Authority

God is a God of order. This is evident from the very beginning of creation. He took a world that was without form and void, covered with darkness, and created an organized, life-sustaining earth. This same God has given order and structure to his kingdom.

> *And he gave some, apostles; and some, prophets; and some, evangelists; and some, pastors and teachers; For the perfecting of the saints, for the work of the ministry, for the edifying of the body of Christ: (Ephesians 4:11-12)*

> *Now ye are the body of Christ, and members in particular. And God hath set some in the church, first apostles, secondarily prophets, thirdly teachers, after that miracles, then gifts of healings, helps, governments, diversities of tongues. (1 Corinthians 12:27-28)*

It is noted that the Lord has given gifts or ministries that are to operate with authority in performing specific roles in the body. He has *"set some in the church"* or he has put, placed, fixed, or appointed individuals in their place of operation or authority in the church. This point is further emphasized by the chosen wording *"first...secondarily...thirdly"*. According to Strong's, *"first"* is an adverb, meaning *"firstly in time, place, order or importance."* It is from the Greek word *protos* meaning *"either in time or place or successions of things or persons"* (Thayer's). Subsequently, *"secondarily"* and *"thirdly"* mean exactly that, second and third in time, place or rank. This is not to debate who has ultimate power or authority, it is to substantiate that the Lord has a structure of authority and He sends, places or sets individuals in specific areas or positions. He empowers individuals, authorizing them to use that power according to His purpose in the area He has sent or set them. When individuals understands this and submits themselves to authority, they can be like the centurion and freely operate within the authority they are given.

Metron

> *"For we dare not make ourselves of the number, or compare ourselves with some that commend themselves: but they measuring themselves by themselves, and comparing themselves among themselves, are not wise. But we will not boast of things without our measure, but according to the measure of the rule which God hath distributed to us, a measure to reach even unto you."*
> *(2 Corinthians 10:12-13.)*

The apostle Paul understood that he had been given a specific area to operate in authority. In the above passage of scripture, Paul speaks of a measure of rule that God has distributed to him. The original Greek gives us a much greater understanding of what he is referencing.

- Measure is the Greek word *metron*, it is *"a determined extent, a portion measured off, a measure or limit"* (Thayer's).

- Rule is *"a definitely bounded or fixed space within the limits of which one's power or influence is confined; it is the province assigned one, or it is one's sphere of activity."* (Thayer's)

Paul was stating that we have a determined portion, a fixed boundary where our rule, influence or authority is to be used. For

Paul, it included the church at Corinth, and he was not concerning himself with the *metron* or area of others. His goal was to see the power of God operate in the area to which he had been sent. Living in Kingdom authority is exercising the delegated authority within the *metron* we are sent to. It is here we are to freely operate with authority according to God's purpose.

If we look to creation, we see this concept of being sent to a specific area from the beginning. Adam, who was created in the image of God, was given dominion, and set in a specific place to operate in authority. *"And the Lord God took the man and put him in the Garden of Eden to tend and guard and keep it" (Genesis 2:15 AMP).* God placed Adam in a particular *metron*, the garden, for the purpose of guarding and tending it. It was here that Adam was to exercise the authority that he had been given.

It is noted that God gave Abram an area to posses. When Israel finally entered the Promised Land they were to exercise authority. God instructed them to drive out the inhabitants and posses the land, promising that He would go with them and fight their battle. Once again, there is the concept of exercising authority in a particular place to which we have been sent.

Giftings Or Graces to Operate In

To this point, the concept of a *metron* of authority has been discussed in the context of being sent to a specific place or to a particular group of people. This was evidenced in the life of Jesus when he stated he was sent to the lost sheep of Israel. The apostle Paul understood he was sent to the Gentiles in general and then to specific churches such as the church of Corinth. It is easy for us to see this exhibited in the lives of many individuals who are in what we referred to as "the ministry". These ministers have particular places, cities, countries or people that they are called or sent to.

However, there is an application of this *metron* that is for every child of God. As stated in chapter two, the apostolic church recognizes the priesthood of every believer. Each born again child of God has been gifted to minister in the body of Christ, using what they have been given so that the body may mature and grow into the image of Jesus Christ. This gifting that each believer is to minister in, carries with it a *metron* of authority.

In the book of Ephesians, prior to describing the ascension gifts of apostle, prophet, evangelist, pastor and teacher, Paul speaks of each of us being given grace according to the measure of the gift of Christ. *But unto every one of us is given grace according to the measure of the gift of Christ. (Ephesians 4:7)* Today's English Version is much clearer: *"Each one of us has received a special gift in proportion to what Christ has given."*

Measure in the KJV text is *metron*. It is telling us that we have been given a grace or special gift, by the grace of Jesus Christ. This grace, or gifting has been given to us to use in the area to which we have been sent. Verse 16 of Ephesians 4 speaks of the body of Christ being joined together and that it is increased *"according to the effectual working in the measure of every part,"* The Weymouth translation says; *"with power proportioned to the need of each individual part."* The word measure here is *metron*. When each part is working in its given power or gifting we can expect the body to increase. Romans 12:6 tells us that each member of the body of Christ is given graces or gifting based on the grace of God. As these gifts are used in the measure or area to which we have been sent, we can anticipate the Lord will reveal Himself, and the body of Christ will be built up.

This idea of a *metron* for the use of our giftings is further revealed as we continue with Romans 12:6. Paul goes on to mention specific graces or giftings that individuals are to operate in; prophesy, ministry, teaching, exhortation, giving, ruling and mercy. These giftings, and many others listed in scripture, are each given a *metron* of authority for their operation. It is the responsibility of each believer to come to an understanding of their spiritual gifts and then find the *metron* of authority where they are to operate.

Let me give a practical example. An individual may know that their gifting is teaching. This gifting can have many areas of application, each good, valid and necessary. The gift of teaching can be used in children's ministry, youth ministry, adult classes, home bible study, cell ministries, prison ministry, nursing home ministry, etc. However, one particular individual may not be an effective teacher in all areas. There may be one ministry that he is much more effective in. This area is their *metron* or area of authority. It is where people are to operate and can expect the authority of God to be manifest. I believe this is the answer to many unfulfilled people who are faithfully ministering in the church today. They are operating outside of their *metron*. Subsequently there is a lack of the intended power and authority. The answer is to find the *metron* where they are to use their giftedness.

Increasing Your Metron

Not boasting of things without our measure, that is, of other men's labours; but having hope, when your faith is increased, that we shall be enlarged by you according to our rule abundantly
(2 Corinthians 10:15)

- The Amplified Bible states; *"our field among you may be greatly enlarged, still within the limits of our commission"*

- The New American Standard Bible states; *"we shall be, within our sphere, enlarged even more by you,"*

The apostle Paul reveals an understanding of operating in a *metron*. This is, as he was successful in using the authority of his *metron*, he expected it to increase. He knew that as the fruit of his ministry became evident, God would enlarge his sphere or rule within the measure or *metron* where he was sent. This truth is applicable to every believer. As we begin to operate our giftings within the measure or *metron* of rule in which we are placed, we can have faith and expect God to increase the measure of rule or authority in which we operate.

Summary

The second key principle in our sentness to operate in Kingdom authority is for each of us to know our *metron* (area of authority). This may be a specific place or people that we are sent to or a particular giftedness that the grace of God has placed within us. Both Jesus and Paul have declared to us that as we begin to operate in the *metron* of authority we have been given, additional authority can be expected. It should be our sincere desire to obtain from the Lord an understanding of our personal gifting and *metron*. Is it a particular geographical place, such as, neighborhood, city, state or place of employment? Is it a particular group of people such as, homeless, singles, divorced, widows, youth, gangs etc.? To effectively operate in Kingdom authority we must actively operate our grace in the place to which we have been sent.

CHAPTER 6
DEVELOPING KINGDOM THINKING

Man's mind, once stretched by a new idea, never regains its original dimensions.
~ Oliver Wendell Holmes

We can summarize the three basic principles of being sent (apostolic) to operate in Kingdom authority as:

1. Being sent with the Lord's authorization to use His power, to fulfill His will.
2. Each of us has been given a specific metron to operate His authority in.
3. The operation of Kingdom authority is based on speaking His will to situations.

The personal challenge for each of us receiving and operating in Kingdom authority is that we must have a mind that is willing to receive the Word of God. We cannot receive this as factual information to file away, nor is it a mental assent or agreement that we can say we understand. To operate in Kingdom authority, we must receive these truths with a mind that has been transformed by the Spirit, allowing us to see from a spiritual perspective. Paul, writing to the church at Rome, discusses the difference between the mind that receives the things of God, and the one that does not.

> *And be not conformed to this world: but be ye transformed by the renewing of your mind, that ye may prove what is that good, and acceptable, and perfect, will of God. (Romans 12:2)*

The hindrance we have to receiving the truth of Kingdom authority is that many have a mind conformed to the philosophies of the world or our church traditions. Overcoming this requires a transforming of our beliefs and values by a renewing of our mind. When we have accomplished this, we will then be able to reveal what the will of God is, manifesting His purpose to creation.

Conforming To The World

In light of Romans 12:2, stated above, Paul admonishes us not be conformed to the world. In my Christian background, I was always led to believe that this referred to the obvious worldly sins. Such actions as immorality, lying, stealing, drunkenness, drugs, abuse and others, have long been preached as worldliness. However, a deeper look at this word reveals much more.

The original Greek word, *suschematizo*, speaks of *"conforming to another's pattern"* (Thayer's). According to Miriam Webster the English word *conform* means: *"to bring into harmony or accord, to be similar or identical, to be in agreement or harmony with, to be obedient or compliant."* So we see that being conformed to the world is not just the sins previously mentioned, it is being shaped after the pattern of the world's value system. It is being in harmony or agreement with the priorities or ways of the world. It is being obedient or compliant to worldly ways and objectives. This lifestyle of the world is opposed to the things of God. Being conformed to the world is living comfortably like the world in its system. Jesus understood the dangers of being conformed to a worldly mindset when he spoke in the parable of the sower *(Mark 4:14-20)*. The attitude of the world is exhibited in the *"cares of this world and the deceitfulness of riches"* and the *"lust of other things"* that choked out the valuable seed of the Word. Because of this focus of a worldly mind, the liberating truths of the Word of God were not able to take root and produce fruit.

Further scriptural evidence of this type of mind not being able to receive the things of God is found in the following texts:

Even the Spirit of truth; whom the world cannot receive, because it seeth him not, neither knoweth him: but ye know him; for he dwelleth with you, and shall be in you. (John 14:17)

But the natural man receiveth not the things of the Spirit of God: for they are foolishness unto him: neither can he know them, because they are spiritually discerned. (1 Corinthians 2:14)

The natural mind, which is conformed to the ways of the world, is unable to receive the things of God. This is because this mind operates from a worldly pattern and cannot grasp or understand the spiritual principles of the mind of God. To this mindset, spiritual truths and their application in life appear to be foolish.

Earlier in his letter to the church at Rome, Paul elaborates on the condition of a conformed mind, and why it cannot receive the things of God. He states, *"For they that are after the flesh do mind the things of the flesh" (Romans 8:5)*. *"After"* the flesh can be translated as *"according to."* According means: *"to cause to conform or agree, a bringing into harmony"* (The Free Dictionary.com). These individuals mind the things of the flesh. Minding is: *"to have an understanding or to direct one's mind to a thing"* (Thayer's). Those who are conformed or in harmony with the fleshly man, have a fleshly understanding: naturally directing their minds to fleshly things. Once again, we are not necessarily speaking of the sinful lifestyle normally associated with the flesh; rather, we are speaking of a mind that looks at things from a natural viewpoint. The truth of the Word of God and situations of life are filtered through a human viewpoint, self-will or self-determination being the ultimate guideline used to accept or reject truth.

Another term that Paul uses to refer to this conformed mind is a carnal mind: *"For to be carnally minded is death;" (Romans 8:6).* Carnal is anything related to the fleshly or worldly appetites and desires rather than toward God. Nelson's Illustrated Bible Dictionary defines carnal as: *"Sensual, worldly, non-spiritual; relating to or given to the crude desires and appetites of the flesh or body. The apostle Paul contrasts 'spiritual people'-that is, those who are under the control of the Holy Spirit-with those who are 'carnal'-those under the control of the flesh."* Nelson's further states that: *"The word carnal is usually reserved in the New Testament to describe worldly Christians."* Paul recognized that the church of Corinth contained many who were carnal, living as spiritual babes; *"And I, brethren, could not speak unto you as unto spiritual, but as unto carnal, even as unto babes in Christ. I have fed you with milk, and not with meat: for hitherto ye were not able to bear it, neither yet now are ye able. For ye are yet carnal: for whereas there is among you envying, and strife, and divisions, are ye not carnal, and walk as men?" (1 Corinthians 3:1-3)*

Paul reveals the seriousness of a carnal mind in Romans 8:7 when he states: *"Because the carnal mind is enmity against God: for it is not subject to the law of God, neither indeed can be".* The New Unger's Bible Dictionary defines enmity as *"deep-rooted hatred or irreconcilable hostility."* Because the carnal mind is motivated by the flesh and rejects the leadership of the Spirit, there is this irreconcilable hostility that will not allow it to receive spiritual truth. It is an enemy, hostile, hating the things of God, and will not be subject or set under the authority of the law of God.

Therefore, it necessitates that we have our minds transformed. We must not allow our values and beliefs to be in harmony and patterned after the worlds system. Operating in Kingdom authority will require us to see from a spiritual perspective, speaking by faith the things that God has already declared accomplished.

The Transformed Mind

> *From that time Jesus began to preach, and to say, Repent: for the kingdom of heaven is at hand. (Matthew 4:17)*

The first message that Jesus preached instructed people to repent because the kingdom of Heaven was near. Strong's definition of repentance is *"to think differently."* Vine's says it is to *"to change one's mind or purpose."* Spiritually speaking, repentance is to have a change or transformation as to how I see my life and my relationship to Jesus. This change of mind or perception will result in a change of my lifestyle.

> *That ye put off concerning the former conversation the old man, which is corrupt according to the deceitful lusts; And be renewed in the spirit of your mind; And that ye put on the new man, which after God is created in righteousness and true holiness. (Ephesians 4:22-24)*

> *And have put on the new man, which is renewed in knowledge after the image of him that created him: (Colossians 3:10)*

True repentance will result in a renewing or a transforming of the mind. The transformation spoken of in Romans 12:2, is from the word *metamorphoo*, or *metamorphais*. It is where we derive our word metamorphosis and it is not just a superficial change, but a change of our nature. This same word is used in regards to Jesus transfiguration on the Mt. of Olives. As Peter, James and John stood by and watched, the Lord was *"transfigured"* before them, revealing His divine nature. In like manner, our minds are to be transfigured, making the very nature of our thoughts and perceptions reveal a divine perspective. Since we are now able to view the situations of life from God's perspective, the truths of the Word of God are able to become tangible to us. Seeing from God's perspective gives us the faith to speak what is already accomplished in the spiritual realm into existence in the temporal world. The transformed mind learns to live life viewed from heaven towards earth.

Proving the Will of God

When our minds are transformed from the carnal, allowing us to see the spiritual, we are then able to *" prove what is that good, and acceptable, and perfect, will of God" (Romans 12:1)*. Again referencing Thayer's definition of being sent, the fourth component speaks of the going and the accomplishment of the purpose as proof an individual had been sent. A mind that is transformed does not just see the natural circumstances, but also sees the spiritual reality of the Word of God. Because of this view, we can prove the will of God because by faith we speak and demonstrate the will of God. Our purpose is to demonstrate that the reality that exists in heaven can be manifest right here and now on earth. We are not just to believe the will of God, we are to put the will of God on display so that others will see and recognize Him. When we speak the will of God, we bring the reality of heaven crashing into the strongholds of this world, proving that there is something greater than man's philosophies by demonstrating a power that is greater than what rules the temporal world. The purpose of a transformed mind and walking in Kingdom authority is not to see what we can do for God, but it is to see what God will do through us as He proves His will when we operate with His authority.

Summary

Operating in Kingdom authority requires a different mindset to receive the things of God. We cannot allow ourselves to be in harmony or alignment with the world's philosophies and priorities. Only when we have a metamorphosis of our way of thinking will we be able to see from a spiritual perspective. Seeing from God's perspective will give us the faith to demonstrate the reality of heaven here and now, resulting in a proof of the will of God. This is the Lord's ultimate purpose for the use of Kingdom authority: that we use it to reveal to this world the power and wonder of Jesus Christ.

CHAPTER 7
DEMONSTRATING KINGDOM AUTHORITY

...because he spoke with authority. Luke 4:32 TEV

Kingdom authority is based on the *apostello* or sending as a special envoy, as a representative of Jesus Christ. It is being endued with His power and authorized to use this power according to His designated purpose. We are each given a measure (*metron*) of rule, be it a particular geographical area, group of people or gifting, in which we are to operate. The next obvious question would be: How are we to exercise this authority we have been given?

Looking to Jesus as our example, we see how He operated in authority. As the Apostle that was sent to a particular place, He exercised spiritual authority by speaking. The message that was declared was not of Himself, but from the one who sent Him.

> *Then said Jesus unto them, When ye have lifted up the Son of man, then shall ye know that I am he, and that I do nothing of myself; but as my Father hath taught me, I speak these things. (John 8:28)*

> *For I have not spoken of myself; but the Father which sent me, he gave me a commandment, what I should say, and what I should speak. (John 12:49)*
>
> *And I know that his commandment is life everlasting: whatsoever I speak therefore, even as the Father said unto me, so I speak. (John 12:50)*
>
> *For I have given unto them the words which thou gavest me; and they have received them, and have known surely that I came out from thee, and they have believed that thou didst send me. (John 17:8)*
>
> *Believest thou not that I am in the Father, and the Father in me? the words that I speak unto you I speak not of myself: but the Father that dwelleth in me, he doeth the works. (John 14:10)*

Jesus understood who had sent him, the purpose for being sent, and the *"metron"* or area He was sent to. He exercised the authority given to Him by speaking the will of the One who sent Him.

Foundation of The Operation of Authority

The Word of God reveals that in the creation process, authority was exercised by speaking. Seven times in Genesis chapter one, it is recorded *"God said"* and following His specific declarations; the words spoken came into existence. This exercise of authority by speaking resulted in the creation of light, the atmosphere, continents, seas, sun, moon, stars and the animals. All were in the mind and will of God, yet to bring them into existence, He needed to speak. The authority in God's spoken word could not be ignored because of His inherent power.

> *So God created man in his own image, in the image of God created he him; male and female created he them. And God blessed them, and God said unto them, Be*

fruitful, and multiply, and replenish the earth, and subdue it: and have dominion over the fish of the sea, and over the fowl of the air, and over every living thing that moveth upon the earth. (Genesis 1:27-28)

In chapter two it was discussed that the purpose of Adam being created in God's image was to exercise dominion or authority over creation. Adam was to use this authority to fill the earth with the image and glory of God. To accomplish this, God needed to give Adam the means to operate or express this authority that he now possessed. One of the unique characteristics of Adam, being made in the image of God, was the ability to speak. Just as God spoke with a purpose, Adam was given the power of speech to fulfill a purpose. Adam was to exercise his authority by speaking to God's creation when the animals were brought to him to see what he would call them.

And out of the ground the LORD God formed every beast of the field, and every fowl of the air; and brought them unto Adam to see what he would call them: and whatsoever Adam called every living creature, that was the name thereof. (Genesis 2:19)

Naming and Authority

The significance of this act is made clear with an examination of the Biblical concept of naming. To be in the position to name something signifies having authority or dominion over it. Through the prophet Isaiah, God speaks to Israel, and declares his sovereignty over them because he called them by name: *"But now thus saith the LORD that created thee, O Jacob, and he that formed thee, O Israel, Fear not: for I have redeemed thee, I have called thee by thy name; thou art mine." (Isaiah 43:1)* Holman Bible Dictionary states that: *"the act of naming implied the power of the namer over the named."*

The most common word of the Old Testament translated call or called is *qara*; it signifies the specification of a name, which is frequently associated with the declaration of sovereignty over it. This is revealed in its first usage: *"And God called the light day, and the darkness he called Night" (Genesis 1:5)*. This is further shown in the Lord's naming of the stars in Psalms 147:4 and Isaiah 40:26 where *"he calleth them all by names."* For the Lord to call the name of a particular part of creation or an individual was His way of proclaiming ownership or lordship. This same power was given to Adam when God brought the animals of creation to be named.

In Genesis 2:19 when God brought the animals to Adam to see what *"he would call them,"* the same word *qara* is used. Here, the language reveals that Adam was exercising authority in naming the animals, just as God named the light, darkness and stars. According to Keil & Delitzsch Commentary on the Old Testament: New Updated Edition, *"by giving them names, Adam was proving himself their Lord."* Vine's Expository Dictionary of Biblical Words states; *"God allowed Adam to 'name' the animals as a concrete demonstration of man's relative sovereignty over them. This act of designated authority was brining them under the dominion of Adam."*

The Scriptures further states in Genesis 2:19 that *"whatsoever Adam called every living creature, that was the name there of."* The original word translated as *"the name there of"* is *shem*, which according to Strong's means: *"a definite and conspicuous position."* According to Dictionary.com, the word definite is defined as; *"clearly defined or determined, having fixed limits."* Conspicuous means being: *"readily visible or observable."* As Adam named the animals he was clearly defining them, putting them in an obvious fixed position in God's order of creation. This was just like God when He called the light by name. *Psalm 74:16* says that; *"thou hast prepared the light and the sun."* The word translated *prepared* means; *"to be set up, to be firmly established, to be fixed"* (Thayer's). Vines further clarifies the meaning of *shem: "This root used concretely connotes being firmly established, being firmly anchored and being firm."* Today's English Version makes this meaning very clear; *"you set the sun and the moon in their places;"* Therefore, this act of naming, performed by both God and Adam, was a designating mark of the individuality of each particular part of creation. Adam was speaking the uniqueness of the animals, consequently, establishing lordship over them by putting them in their specific place in creation.

Adam's Fall & The Restoration of Authority

From the beginning we see that God expressed His power and authority by speaking. This ability to operate in authority was passed on to the one created in God's image, Adam. Unfortunately, due to Adams fall, he lost the ability to exercise authority. Subsequently this has been passed on to each generation of his descendants. For God to fulfill His purpose of the earth being filled with His image and glory, there necessitated a plan to restore man to a place of authority. This was accomplished through the ministry of Jesus Christ.

The restoration of authority began with the coming of Jesus Christ. He was the manifest or revealed image of God, and was sent as the Apostle to do the will of the One who sent Him. To accomplish this, the words that He spoke were not His own, but the one who dwelt in Him *(John 12:49, 14:10)*. Once again we see the exercise of authority by speaking.

Jesus came as the Last Adam to restore what the first Adam lost: authority and dominion. The transformation of man's fallen nature is essential for the restoration of authority. The word of God tells us that; *"as we have borne the image of the earthy, we shall also bear the image of the heavenly (1 Corinthians 15:49).* We are to *"put on the new man, which is renewed in knowledge after the image of him that created him" (Colossians 3:10).* Just as in our fallen and unsaved nature, we bear the image of Adam; in our born again nature, Jesus created the opportunity for us to bear His image. Romans 8:29 states that: *"For whom he did foreknow, he also did predestinate to be conformed to the image of his Son."* This is not to say that God has predetermined who would be saved. However as an omniscient God we must believe that He knows who would accept the grace provided and become born again of the water and the spirit *(John 3:5)*. The Gospel of Jesus Christ, which is His death, burial and resurrection, is applied to our lives when we repent and in obedience are baptized in His name and by faith filled with His Spirit. These that were born again, He did predetermine that they should be conformed to the image of his Son, Jesus. The purpose of being born again is to renew us spiritually after the image of the one who created us, restoring us to the place of authority and dominion that was originally given to Adam. What a wonderful revelation for each of us to know that we have been chosen by God to bear His image. We have been elected to walk in His authority and empowered to use his *dunamis* to fulfill his purpose. He has clearly shown us that to do this we must speak His will into existence.

The Faith of The Centurion

We return to the Centurion of Luke 7. How did he exercise his authority? Was it by his physical ability or his mental acuity? No. He exercised his authority by speaking. Because he understood a higher authority set him in a specific place, to perform the purpose of that authority, he was able to speak with authority. His faith to speak was centered in the power of the Roman government. It was based on his understanding that as the representative of Rome, he was supported by the power of Rome and as long as he fulfilled the purpose of Rome, he could speak commands with faith. In fact, that was Jesus comment, that he had not see so great a faith. The Centurion's faith came not from knowing his purpose or place, but from knowing who it was that sent him. It is the same in Kingdom authority. My faith is not in the authority I have, nor even in the miraculous results this authority brings; Kingdom authority ALWAYS returns my faith back to the one who sent me, Jesus Christ.

Speaking the Will of God

> *As every man hath received the gift, even so minister the same one to another, as good stewards of the manifold grace of God. If any man speak, let him speak as the oracles of God; if any man minister, let him do it as of the ability which God giveth: that God in all things may be glorified through Jesus Christ, to whom be praise and dominion for ever and ever. Amen. (1 Peter 4:10-11)*

Peter speaking of ministering with the gifts we each have received states: *"If any man speak, let him speak as the oracles of God;" (1 Peter 4:11)*. In this verse, *"the oracles"*, *"the"* is not in the original text. *Oracles* is from *logion*, and means utterance. The statement *"of God"* is from one word *theos*. Therefore this statement could read: *"if any man speak, let him speak as utterance God, or as the utterance of God."* Peter is referencing that we have been given the ministry to speak the things of God.

In John chapter 17, there is a rich vein of truth in reference to disciples receiving and speaking the Word of God. Verse 18 has been discussed earlier; this is Jesus' statement that in the same way He was sent into the world, He was now sending His disciples into the world. This means in the same manner He came speaking the Word of God, He was now expecting the disciples to go and speak the Word of God. The following verses clarify that we have been given His words to go and speak:

> *For I have given unto them the words which thou gavest me; and they have received them, and have known surely that I came out from thee, and they have believed that thou didst send me. (John 17:8)*

> *I have given them thy word; and the world hath hated them, because they are not of the world, even as I am not of the world. (John 17:14)*

Neither pray I for these alone, but for them also which shall believe on me through their word; (John 17:20)

Being sent as the Apostle, Jesus received the words to speak from the One who sent Him. Subsequently, it is His intention that we are to take these same words that He received, and speak them to the world. His prayer was for those that would believe on Him through these words that were spoken. We should begin to operate with faith, speaking the will of God, knowing that it is His desire that it would impact those who hear.

Power in the Word

In their respective ministries, Jesus and the disciples were seen declaring the will of God to situations they encountered. In ministering to the needs of individuals, they did not pray and ask God to do what His word said was already finished. The reason God's word in creation was so powerful resulting in what was spoken coming into existence, is because it was already accomplished in His mind.

In the beginning was the Word, and the Word was with God, and the Word was God. (John 1:1)

John 1:1 is a key to understanding the power of speaking the will or word of God. Three times in this text the word *logos* is translated Word and it is used 323 times in the rest of the New Testament, many times in reference to what Jesus was speaking. Strong's defines *logos* as; *"something said, including the thought."*

- Vine's state that *logos* is; *"'a word,' as embodying a conception or idea, denotes among its various meanings, 'a saying, statement or declaration,' uttered"* or *"the expression of thought."*
- Vincent's Word Studies gives the following insight into the meaning of *logos*; *"It therefore signifies both the*

outward form by which the inward thought is expressed, and the inward thought itself."

Logos is more than the act of vocalizing; it includes with it the revelation of the thought or intent of the one speaking. There cannot be a separation of the word spoken and the essence or nature of the one speaking. In fact, the last part of John 1:1 clearly shows this; *"and the Word was God."* I personally like how the Amplified Bible states it; *"and the Word was God Himself."* When *"God said"* it was not a mere vocalizing of word, but it was a revealing of the mind of God. He was speaking into tangible existence what had already been accomplished in His mind.

When we speak the Word of God, we are speaking or declaring what He has already accomplished in His mind. When Jesus and the disciples spoke to situations, they declared the existing spiritual truth to be real in the here and now. Time and space prevents us here from examining every miracle performed by the Lord, however if you will make it a point to examine each instance, you will see that Jesus "just" spoke or declared the truth of will of God. For three and one half years the disciples watched His example, it was natural for them to follow His pattern of ministry. Taking the time to examine the miracles performed by the disciples will reveal, that they did not pray for God to do something, they spoke the spiritual reality into existence. The disciples had grasped the third principle of Kingdom authority; by speaking the will of God to the situations of life they encountered, they exercised a bold faith to believe that what the Word of God said, it meant.

Speaking The Will of God Now

When the disciples asked the Lord to show them how to pray, Jesus gave them the principles to declare the will of God. His response to their inquiry in Luke 11:2 was pray (or speak this way):

- *"thy kingdom come"* – Young's Literal Translations says *"thy reign come."* They were to pray or speak the reign or dominion of the Kingdom here and now.

- *"thy will be done, as in heaven, so in earth."* – they were to speak His will, as it was performed in heaven, it should be performed here on earth.

So much could be written about the will of God that is available for us to experience now. The Word of God contains the mind of God toward His people, proclaiming the power and privilege that they should walk with. His word has promised power, healing, deliverance, miracles, transformation of the mind, peace, joy, strength, direction and much more. It is the Lord's desire that we as His disciples speak the will of His kingdom into the lives of individuals. In John 14:12, Jesus tells us that; *"He that believeth on me, the works that I do shall he do also; and greater works than these shall he do;"* It is His desire that we minister in the same manner as He did, as evidenced by His words in John 17:18: *"As thou hast sent me into the world, even so have I also sent them into the world."*

Practical Application

When instructing groups in the truths of Living In Kingdom Authority, we end the series with a high note of faith, allowing the people to step out and demonstrate Kingdom authority. For many, it is the first time God uses them in the miraculous. For others, it may be the first time they have witnessed God's miraculous power at work.

Before the people step out in faith, we set the foundation of one way (not the only) to operate with faith. The following is a typical description of what we do and say.

First a call is made for those who have a disease, sickness or ailment in their body, based on two requirements. One, they believe God is a healer and wants to heal them. Two, they, themselves want to be healed! I know, it may seem crazy, but there are people who do not want to be healed because they can lose what we call in the healthcare field, secondary gain. These are things like a disability check or the pampering they get from others. So I tell them, by coming to the front, you are stating that you want God to heal you. Then we call for believers, those who believe God can heal and wants to use them to be the vessel of the miraculous. I have them pair up with those needing healing.

In the next step, I have those needing healing, to describe in one or two words their disease or sickness. Now this is significant, I have learned by experience, if someone needs to tell you a looooong story about their problem, it usually means they have taken ownership of it. This can make it very hard for them to receive their healing. Also, I comment on using terminology such as *"my_____"* (you fill in the disease). This verbiage, again, usually means ownership of the disease or ailment.

Then at this time, a question is posed: "How many of you had your condition diagnosed by a physician?" To me, this is another faith obstacle to be addressed.

To a physician, a diagnosis is naming a set of symptoms and test results. It allows them to put a handle on it and prescribe some form of treatment. What I want to emphasize is that it is a naming! Remember our discussion on naming? It is an exercise of authority. It is my belief, that when a doctor gives us a diagnosis, it is our nature to submit to their authority and receive it. I have known individuals and know people who have known others that went to a doctor for a check up or because they had just a small symptom. After the exam and test, the doctor said: "I am sorry you have…(many times cancer)" and the individual passed away in less than 6 months. Now I am not implying we deny the problem, I am just cautioning us against whose authority we submit ourselves to.

To those whose condition has been diagnosed by a physician, we present these scriptures:

(Jesus is) *Far above all principality, and power, and might, and dominion, and **every name that is named**, not only in this world, but also in that which is to come (Emphasis added, Ephesians 1:21)*

*Wherefore God also hath highly exalted him, and given him **a name which is above every name**. (Emphasis added, Philippians 2:9)*

I want them to grasp that no matter who named their condition, the name of Jesus has more power and is above the name of any disease processes!

Then in the final step, I instruct those praying to lay hands on the people and take authority in the name of Jesus and speak to the conditions. It is not some magic mantra to recite, but has two fundamental components: first it is declaring the name of Jesus and it is speaking with authority over the condition.

It is usually at this point, the power of the Lord begins to manifest and the miraculous happens. I could fill up pages of the testimonies of the conditions that are gone after the people take authority. I have listed some of the stories of healings in the last chapter to help build your faith.

Summary

From the beginning, God exercised His authority by speaking. The words that He spoke contained power because they were already accomplished in His mind. The power to speak with the same authority was given to Adam to exercise the will of God. After the fall of Adam, Jesus restored this right for His disciples. When we are born again, and we speak the will of God into situations of life, we can expect there to be miraculous results. Just as Jesus was sent to exercise dominion and manifest God, we as born again children of God have also been sent. We exercise this same authority Jesus used when, by faith, we speak the will of God

CHAPTER 8
THE KINGDOM MODEL OF DISCIPLESHIP

The decision to grow always involves a choice between risk and comfort. This means that to be a follower of Jesus you must renounce comfort as the ultimate value of your life. ~ John Ortberg

And Jesus came and spoke to them, saying, "All authority has been given to Me in heaven and on earth. Go therefore and make disciples of all the nations, baptizing them in the name of the Father and of the Son and of the Holy Spirit, teaching them to observe all things that I have commanded you; and lo, I am with you always, even to the end of the age. Amen. Matthew 28:18-20 NKJV

Kingdom authority has at its foundation the understanding that all authority exists with Jesus, and we are not advocating an operation of authority outside of an intimate relationship with Him. In fact, if there is a separation, there is no longer a sending, resulting in a forfeiture of the authority to use His power.

However, if we acknowledge the source of the authority and power, exercising it according to His purpose and plan, we can expect the Lord to perform the miraculous.

In Matthew 28:18, the Lord reminded the disciples of the source of the authority they were sent to use, along with its purpose, to make disciples. This process of making disciples was to begin with the new birth experience, followed by teaching or instructing the new believers in the commands of the Lord. As they strove to be obedient to this purpose, Jesus promised that He would be with them until the end of the age.

Since Jesus is the King Apostle, and it is His will for us to make disciples, examining how He mentored the twelve reveals a model of Kingdom discipleship consisting of four progressive steps. These steps include: a Calling, Instruction, Empowering and a Sending. In His three and one half years of ministry, Jesus exemplified this model as He interacted with the disciples. Examining these four points of His model reveals a method that will work today in raising up disciples who are equipped to walk and minister in apostolic authority.

1. The Calling

The initial step in becoming a disciple of Jesus Christ is the personal calling each individual receives. In John chapter 3, there is a dialogue between Jesus and a religious leader of the Jews, a Pharisee named Nicodemus. It begins with Nicodemus coming to Jesus inquiring about the power in which Jesus ministers. As a religious leader, one who was knowledgeable in the ways of God, he recognized that the authority Jesus operated in could only be of God. This realization prompted him to seek out the Lord. Jesus responds to Nicodemus' inquiry by instructing him in how he might come to his own grasp of this authority. In verses five and seven, Jesus says that Nicodemus must be *"born again of the water and the spirit"* if he is to *"see"* or *"enter"* the kingdom of Heaven. The same applies to individuals today – the new birth experience is the initial response to His calling.

Subsequent to the born-again experience, discipleship is the key. This calling of discipleship is an invitation to be involved with Jesus in the promotion of the kingdom of Heaven. Discipleship is by the invitation of Jesus, we have not chosen Him, but He has chosen us. Within this call, Jesus is offering us a mentoring relationship intended to prepare us for the ministry that He has chosen us for.

This calling to discipleship consists of two key elements: First there is a call to separate ourselves **from** our present way of life. Second, there is a call to separate ourselves **to** a particular way of life. This calling is asking us to leave our old way of viewing life, and to embrace a new heavenly way of life with its priorities and purposes. It is a repenting of our self-rule, and a transforming of our minds to a kingdom view.

A Separation From

And when he had gone a little further thence, he saw James the son of Zebedee, and John his brother, who also were in the ship mending their nets. And straightway he called them: and they left their father Zebedee in the ship with the hired servants, and went after him. (Mark 1:19-20)

And Jesus, walking by the sea of Galilee, saw two brethren, Simon called Peter, and Andrew his brother, casting a net into the sea: for they were fishers. And he saith unto them, Follow me, and I will make you fishers of men. And they straightway left their nets, and followed him. And going on from thence, he saw other two brethren, James the son of Zebedee, and John his brother, in a ship with Zebedee their father, mending their nets; and he called them. And theimmediately left the ship and their father, and followed him. (Matthew 4:18-22)

In the above texts, we see Jesus is calling four of His disciples. In this calling Jesus was asking them to leave their current life, follow Him and He would make them into what He desired. The Amplified Bible, in Mark 1:20, states that James and John's response was *"an abandoning of all mutual claims."* They made a choice to abandon all claims to an inheritance from dad's business. Jesus' call was to leave everything that was comfortable, familiar, reliable, stable and sure to follow, by faith, where He would take them. Later on, Peter acknowledged this separation they had made when he spoke to the Lord, saying: *"Then Peter began to say unto him, Lo, we have left all, and have followed thee" (Mark 10:28).* Jesus' call to discipleship is a radical call. It is not one to be entered half-heartedly, but it is one of total commitment. It is a call that can only be answered by faith, leaving the familiar, not looking back, forsaking those things that are behind, and looking to Him for direction.

The call of discipleship cannot be proven unless our lives reveal a distinct separation from our old way of living, both temporal and spiritual. This separation can require us to reexamine and possibly leave behind traditional spiritual views that have become too comfortable. Frederick B. Wilcox is quoted as saying; *"You can't steal second base and keep your foot on first."* The truth expressed in this statement is that to get to a new place it requires the leaving of the comfort and security of the current location. So it is in living for God, if we are ever going to live in Kingdom authority, to go to the place of authority, we must leave where we currently live spiritually.

Abrams Call

Examining the calling of Abram, this principle of being called from our current place becomes apparent. *"Now the LORD had said unto Abram, Get thee out of thy country, and from thy kindred, and from thy father's house, unto a land that I will shew thee:" (Genesis 12:1).* For Abram to posses the promises given to him by the Lord, it was necessary that he first leave some things behind. These were not easy things to leave, his country, and relatives, even his father's house. It was a call for Abram to separate from his present world with all its familiarity and comfort of routine. This was necessary because God knew there were ties that would bind him. Abrams familiarity with his surroundings and the opinions of relatives or friends would challenge the direction he was hearing from God, threatening to undermine his faith and obedience. Therefore, it necessitated that for Abram to enter the place God had for him; he must first leave his current situation.

The calling to apostolic discipleship requires each of us to exercise faith by leaving behind the familiar things that would hinder our ability to perceive the direction of Lord. We have already stated the greatest hindrance to apostolic authority is the traditions of man that we hold. Therefore as born again believers we must separate from these hindrances, freeing ourselves to follow the leading of the Lord. Unfortunately, many times when an individual steps into the realm of the Spirit, there are those who will question their actions. Many well meaning traditional saints challenge the necessity of such a dramatic commitment. The reality is that we must be willing to leave behind anything that is close enough to us that would hinder our faith and obedience to where the Lord is leading us.

A Separation To

Answering the call of the Lord to walk in apostolic authority not only involves a separation from an old way of life, but also includes a separation **to** a new life of obedience and faith. The Lord does not ask us just to give up the familiar, but He desires that we separate from the familiar so he can lead us to a new place in Him spiritually. When Abram was instructed to leave his country and family, the Lord then asked him to go to a land that He would show him. Abram's calling was not complete when he left, but was complete when he chose to follow to the land the Lord would lead him to.

The challenge of answering the calling is that much of the time we focus on what we must leave behind or give up. We fail to realize that it is more than a separation **from**, but it is a separation **to** something and *Someone*. We are like Lot's wife and desire to look back at the familiar rather than by faith continuing to look forward. Much like Israel did in the wilderness, we long again for the familiar leeks and onions of our limited existence, rather than anticipate with excitement and faith the promises of God. Many times we fail to see that the Lord's calling is to a greater place than where we now exist.

In Matthew 4:19, when Jesus called Peter and Andrew, He said *"Follow me."* The place we are called to is specific, it is to follow Jesus. In Matthew 4:22, it gives the response of James and John when Jesus called them: *"And they immediately left the ship and their father, and followed him."* The Amplified says: *"joining Him as disciples and siding with His party."* The word *followed* in verse 22 means *"a follower"* or *"companion"* (Vines). The disciples left their current life, to become companions with Jesus. They were in a union or unity that resulted in going the same direction as the Lord. The calling of the Lord is to join Him as a companion, to walk in unity with Him as He leads. It is a calling to an intimate relationship where we become like Him and walk in His ways. This calling is to a way of life, a journey that will fulfill the purpose of His kingdom.

A Calling To Become

Jesus' call to separate ourselves from our old life and to Him is not to bring us to a place of stagnation and spiritual isolation; it is a call to become all that we can be. When the Lord called Abram, it was a calling with a promise that he would become something special in the plan of God: *"He promised Abram I will make of thee a great nation" (Genesis 12:2)*. Abram was not to remain the same as he followed God, but he would receive blessings and enter into a special relationship. He was promised a destiny that would far outlast his temporal life. Jesus' promise to the disciples was *"I will make you fishers of men."* They were promised that if they followed Him, they would be fashioned and formed for a special ministry. Jesus came to impact this world, He came to reveal the kingdom of Heaven, and He called His disciples to be His companions. He is issuing the same call to each of us today, to become His companion as we impact our world.

2. Instruction

And Jesus went about all Galilee, teaching in their synagogues, and preaching the gospel of the kingdom, and healing all manner of sickness and all manner of disease among the people. (Matthew 4:23)

In the process of learning, one of the best methods is to learn from one who is already proficient in the subject. This is evident in the second point of Kingdom discipleship that Jesus modeled as he traveled, teaching and preaching the gospel of the Kingdom. In Matthew 4:23, *teaching* is defined as: *"to know or teach, it includes the aim of shaping of the will of the pupil"* (Lexical Aids To The New Testament, The Hebrew-Greek Key Study Bible, AMG Publishers). Jesus' purpose of instruction was to impart a knowledge that would bring about a change in those who heard Him, shaping their will and purpose. According to Dictionary.com teaching is comprised of three parts. First, it is to impart knowledge or skill. Second, it is to condition to a certain action or frame of mind. Third, it is to cause to learn by example or experience.

Therefore, the purpose of teaching is to condition the student to a certain frame of mind, imparting knowledge and skills by example or experience. Jesus did just this as He spent three and one half years with the disciples. During this time, His teaching and ministry conditioned them to a particular frame of mind, one that viewed situations from a Kingdom perspective. His instruction imparted unto them knowledge and skills in the operation of Kingdom principles through the power of His Spirit. Not only did He give them knowledge, but also in the daily life of His ministry, Jesus exemplified this lifestyle of authority as He performed signs and wonders.

The intended purpose of instruction in Kingdom discipleship is to bring about a change in the thoughts and will of the disciple, which will produce a lifestyle that demonstrates Kingdom authority. This is accomplished by instructing disciples in the beliefs, values and culture of the Kingdom to the place that it results in a kingdom mindset. A mind that has been transformed to kingdom values will result in a Kingdom lifestyle, revealing the authority and power of the King.

> *And he gave some, apostles; and some, prophets; and some, evangelists; and some, pastors and teachers; For the perfecting of the saints, for the work of the ministry, for the edifying of the body of Christ: Till we all come in the unity of the faith, and of the knowledge of the Son of God, unto a perfect man, unto the measure of the stature of the fulness of Christ: (Ephesians 4:11-13)*

It is still the Lord's intent that disciples are instructed in the ways of His kingdom. Paul writing to the church at Ephesus identified the five fold ascension gift ministries as those that were given to instruct or equip the saints. Verse twelve in The Amplified Bible states: *"His intention was the perfecting and the full equipping of the saints (His consecrated people), [that they should do] the work of ministering toward building up Christ's body (the church)."* The primary responsibility of the ascension gift ministries is a completing of the saints, furnishing them with the understanding of the ministry gifts that has been placed in them. The believers are then to be sent into the body to use these giftings to build up the body of Christ. This same responsibility has been passed on to the leadership of the church today. It should be the single purpose of each leader to fully equip the members in how to operate their giftedness in apostolic authority, allowing the body of Christ, which is the church, to be built up and manifest the glory of God to this world.

3. Empowerment

It has been said, "knowledge is power." However, having information about something does not give us power, but it is the correct application of this knowledge that can be powerful. In the New Testament, the English word knowledge is used 52 times. Of these, the Greek word *epignosis* is used 21 times, and according to Vines it means: *"exact or full knowledge, discernment, recognition,' it expressing a fuller or a full 'knowledge,' a greater participation by the 'knower' in the object 'known,' thus more powerfully influencing him."* The knowledge received from instruction is not to be solely an accumulation of facts and information, but it should involve a relationship and participation between the one doing the knowing and what is known. In short, the one learning must experience the proper application or usage of the knowledge. In the case of apostolic authority, it requires that we come into an intimate relationship with the one who has instructed us, Jesus Himself.

Jesus understood that the teaching of Kingdom principles alone was not enough. On at least two occasions, he sent out groups of disciples to experience or practice what they had been taught.

> *And when he had called unto him his twelve disciples, he gave them power against unclean spirits, to cast them out, and to heal all manner of sickness and all manner of disease. (Matthew 10:1)*

> *After these things the Lord appointed other seventy also, and sent them two and two before his face into every city and place, whither he himself would come. (Luke 10:1)*

Not only did He empower them, but you will find in subsequent text, that He specified where they were to go, who they were to speak to and how they were to respond to various situations. In the second instance, we again see the Lord empowering disciples. He gives them instructions, and sends them on their mission. It is significant to note that He sent them; sent here is *apostello*. He sent them out as His representatives, to speak his word to accomplish his mission.

The result: *"And the seventy returned again with joy, saying, Lord, even the devils are subject unto us through thy name" (Luke 10:17).* They returned and gave an account to Jesus of how they were able to operate in the authority that He had modeled and given to them.

A third example of the Lord's empowering is found in the life of the Apostle Paul. In his letter to Timothy he speaks of the empowerment he received from the Lord: *"And I thank Christ Jesus our Lord, who hath enabled me, for that he counted me faithful, putting me into the ministry;"* Paul was grateful because the Lord had enabled him. This is the Greek word *endunamoo*, which means, *"to empower"* (Strong's). Paul recognized that there was an empowerment or an enabling in his ministry that was of a supernatural origin. It was this enabling that allowed him to minister in the manner that he did.

The life that answers the call of the Lord and embraces the instructions in Kingdom principles will receive an empowering of the Spirit of the Lord. Apostolic authority is acting by faith with the knowledge we have been instructed, knowing that Jesus Christ is the one who empowers us.

4. Sending

The ultimate goal of discipleship is to have mature followers who are able to make new disciples. This was evident in Jesus' commissioning of His followers:

> *And Jesus came and spake unto them, saying, All power is given unto me in heaven and in earth. Go ye therefore, and teach all nations, baptizing them in the name of the Father, and of the Son, and of the Holy*

Ghost: Teaching them to observe all things whatsoever I have commanded you: and, lo, I am with you alway, even unto the end of the world. Amen (Matthew 28:18-29).

Jesus is sending His disciples to repeat the Kingdom model of discipleship: go to the nations, call them via the new birth experience, and instruct them in how to become disciples.

Sending is the final step in Kingdom discipleship. Once individuals answer the call, are instructed, and realize their empowerment and how the Lord intends them to use it, they are then sent out to minister their giftedness. The root word of apostle or apostleship means *"one who is sent."* Jesus tells us in John 17:18 that we are sent just as He was sent. It is the Lord's desire to have mature disciples who have separated themselves to His cause and are operating in His authority accomplishing the mission of proclaiming the kingdom of Heaven and His glory. This is the basis of the scriptural promises that are given to us as His disciples:

> *And these signs shall follow them that believe; In my name shall they cast out devils; they shall speak with new tongues; They shall take up serpents; and if they drink any deadly thing, it shall not hurt them; they shall lay hands on the sick, and they shall recover. (Mark 16:17-18)*

> *Verily, verily, I say unto you, He that believeth on me, the works that I do shall he do also; and greater works than these shall he do; because I go unto my Father. And whatsoever ye shall ask in my name, that will I do, that the Father may be glorified in the Son. (John 14:12-13)*

> *Jesus answered and said unto them, Verily I say unto you, If ye have faith, and doubt not, ye shall not only do this which is done to the fig tree, but also if ye shall*

say unto this mountain, Be thou removed, and be thou cast into the sea; it shall be done. And all things, whatsoever ye shall ask in prayer, believing, ye shall receive. (Matthew 21:21-22)

The purpose of Kingdom discipleship is to get us to the place that we are acting as His image on this earth, fulfilling His original purpose – that the earth might be filled with the image and glory of God.

Summary

We are given apostolic authority with the mandate to go and make disciples. As we make disciples, we are reproducing the image of God as was intended from creation.

The Kingdom model for the making of disciples consists of four stages: First, there is the answering of the call to separation. We are to separate ourselves **from** the things that would hinder us, while separating ourselves **to** the Lord and His purpose. Secondly, there is the instruction of those that are called, detailing what it means to be a disciple and how to operate within the giftings given by God. Thirdly, is the empowerment of each individual to effectively demonstrate Kingdom authority. And finally, there is the sending of the disciple to their appropriate place(s) of ministry within the body. Kingdom discipleship is the method by which the church today can fulfill the mandate given to Adam at his creation, to be fruitful, multiply and replenish the earth.

CHAPTER 9
YOUR RESOURCES & KINGDOM AUTHORITY

What I possess, God owns. ~ Howard Dayton

The world asks, 'What does a man own?' Christ asks, 'How does he use it? ~ Andrew Murray

It is a wonderful thing to be part of the Kingdom of God. Our place as sent representatives to express His image is one of the most privileged responsibilities to have. Living in Kingdom authority requires a Kingdom lifestyle of faithfulness: not just to doctrinal obedience, but faithfulness in our stewardship of His financial resources. This is the life that will find itself rewarded with more authority. To receive more, we must be faithful, diligent, effective, and responsible with what have been given.

This truth is revealed to us in two parables: The Parables of the Talents and The Parable of the Pounds. To further expand this truth and application to our lives we will look at the Parable of the Talents, found in Matthew 24:14-30.

The Story Trailer

Lets start with a story trailer. Jesus as the master storyteller lays the foundation of Kingdom truths. He tells us the Kingdom is like this man who calls his servants together and gives them each a certain amount of resources to be responsible for; then he leaves.

Upon his return, he conducts an audit, asking each servant to give an account of what they had accomplished with his resources. Two of the servants did a great job of investing and doubled their resources, while the third, just protected what he had received.

Because of their faithfulness, the two successful servants were made *"ruler over many things."* Unfortunately, the third servant was considered wicked and unprofitable. His "reward" was to be cast from the owner's presence.

UnPacking The Parable

Before we delve into this parable, we need to establish its framework. Matthew chapter 25 is a continuation of Jesus answer to the disciple's question of his return posed in chapter 24. It is the second parable of chapter 25 – the 1st is commonly called the Parable of the Ten Virgins. Jesus launches this discourse with a statement signifying that this parable is an example of the Kingdom. He says in verse 1, *"The kingdom of heaven shall be likened to..."* Then proceeds to present the parable of the virgins and bridegrooms return.

The KJV begins the Parable of the Talents in verse 14 with the words *"for the kingdom of heaven."* This was added by the translators, but based on context it is appropriate.

The following is from the Amplified Bible; I have removed the comments and clarifications. It is my purpose here to show the natural flow of the text. *"Watch therefore, for you know neither the day nor the hour when the Son of Man will come. For it is like a man who was about to take a long journey, and he called his servants together and entrusted them with his property"(vs 13, 14).* From this version, we can see that Jesus was flowing from the parable of the ten virgins as a Kingdom example, into the next one regarding the servants and the use of their owner's talents.

So from this, I believe we are on a solid footing to say that this is another illustration of Kingdom principles. With that context, lets begin to break it down.

It's a Kingdom Thing

This parable starts with some obvious but deemphasized truths, the greatest being; this is what the Kingdom is like! This is crucial for us to grasp, this is not an option or suggestion, it is an example of Kingdom principles and their demonstration and manifestation. The implied truth here is that if I am in the Kingdom, this is the conduct I will express in my lifestyle.

A kingdom is a place where the rule and reign of the king exists. It is NOT a democracy, republic, communism, or socialism. It is the king's word that determines what is appropriate. It is from the king that all rights, privileges and authority are derived. In short, the only rights a person would have are that which the king says they have.

Along with this kingdom context we see that Jesus is setting up this parable as an illustration as to how it is in the Kingdom. He is implying there are kingdom principles that will be exhibited in a particular lifestyle of the inhabitants of His kingdom. From this, we can see what the King expects and inspects.

Who's Got The Goods?

For the kingdom of heaven is as a man travelling into a far country, who called his own servants, and delivered unto them his goods. (Matthew 25:14)

Now that we have set the context, lets continue and delve into some details in this verse.

First, this man who was about to take a trip, called to him *"his own servants."* The Greek here is *doulos* and means *"a slave, bondman, man of servile condition"* (Thayer's). Thayer's further adds that it is metaphorically used of someone *"who gives himself up wholly to another's will"* or *"devoted to another to the disregard of one's own interests."* It says they were his *"own."* What this speaks to us is a sense of relationship and familiarity. This man obviously knew these servants. Trusting them with his wealth indicates that he had knowledge of their character and abilities.

Second, they were servants. The purpose of a servant is to do what the master instructs: putting his will ahead of their own. The main purpose of the servant is to see that the master's well being is taken care of. They are to be a steward of the master's things.

This leads us to the third point: this man delivered to them *"his goods."* The servants were not entrusted with community property or were they given gifts to use, they were given property that belonged to the master. As we shall see later, I believe the master expected his goods to be treated in a way that revealed they understood who owned them.

Application

Bringing this verse into our modern life confronts head on one of the greatest strongholds in our lives: that being our self and control. The simple yet profoundly challenging truth is that the master is an illustration of God and how our relationship to him should be. He is the owner, they are His goods and we are to be his faithful servants! Thus, he has the right to give the directives and expect obedience from us.

One of the greatest challenges we face in our spiritual lives is dealing with ownership. In North America, our culture is one of individualism: we tend to view money and material possessions as individual property. Therefore, since I own it, I have the right to use it as I see fit. We strongly resist someone telling us what to do with our stuff.

However, if we are to live in the Kingdom and demonstrate His authority, we must grasp the truth Jesus is presenting in the introduction to this parable: this is THE WAY of the Kingdom. The King is the source of everything and we are his servants, not the owners. It is our responsibility to use the resources of our king in a manner that is conducive to His purposes, not ours.

Somehow our concepts of faithful stewardship have been diminished, at best, to the tithe. We feel that if we consistently give 10%, we are being good stewards. Unfortunately, this was not the purpose of the tithe: it was meant to be a reminder that God was the owner and source of everything. I believe in this parable, Jesus was reminding the listeners who their source was.

The Nature Of His Goods

And unto one he gave five talents, to another two, and to another one; (Matthew 25:15)

At this point I want to address a misconception, at least one I had for years, as to the nature of the goods that were distributed. In verse 15, Jesus describes what was given to each of the three servants. The first received five talents, the second two and the third received one talent.

In my 30+ yrs of church involvement, I have always heard it referenced that the talents here were associated with the servants' abilities or giftings. I have heard sermons and unfortunately early on myself, ministered that we needed to use our talents or abilities in a way that profited the Kingdom or was pleasing to God. I have looked at many different commentaries and while they will acknowledge the literal meaning for the word talent, most make the application of truth the using of our gifts or abilities. Yet when

I stop to examine the text unbiasedly, I see that is not what is meant.

At this place, don't misunderstand me; I am not saying we do not need to use our giftings for the Kingdom. There are numerous texts that support the correct usage of our spiritual gifts and abilities. I am just saying, this is not the meaning of the word talent, and in my opinion, the application of the word for this parable.

So What Is A Talent?

So what was the talent? According to various sources, a talent was a balance (Strong's) or unit of weight, used in measuring out a particular sum of money (Vine's). A talent is approximately the mass of water necessary to fill an amphora, which is 1 cubic foot or around 130 lbs.[1] Later it came to mean something weighed, a weight, and hence a talent as a certain fixed weight for gold and silver.

The talent was also used as a denomination for money, which was reckoned by weight. Different sums of local currency were attributed to each monetary talent. It is now estimated that a talent was equal to approximately one thousand dollars. Whatever its exact value, in the New Testament a talent indicates a large sum of money

So in short, each servant was given a measured out sum of MONEY! Now I am not going to get into determining the dollar value of each talent, I think just us recognizing it was money is good enough to get the point across.

How Much Can You Handle?

...to every man according to his several ability; and straightway took his journey. (Matthew 25:15)

---

[1] Wikipedia http://en.wikipedia.org/wiki/Talent_(measurement)

Now that we have identified the talent as literal money, it opens up the next statement in verse 15, which is: *"to every man according to his several ability."* The Amplified Bible states that each received *"... in proportion to his own personal ability."* So the amount of money each servant received was based on his or her individual ability. This is quite revealing.

The master was watching his servants; he obviously knew what they could handle. This speaks of a relationship that existed between the owner and his servants. He was familiar with how they handled their lives and responsibilities and this revealed to the master what they could each handle.

We are given His wealth FOR His purpose

God still works the same today. We receive based on our abilities or dare I say faithfulness demonstrated in our daily life. It is my belief that our level of stewardship over our stuff will determine the level or amount we will receive. He will not trust us with more than we are able to handle.

The challenging truth is that it is very possible, that the amount of money you bring home now, is because that is all you have proven by your stewardship that you are able to handle.

The Audit

After a long time the lord of those servants cometh, and reckoneth with them. (Matthew 25:19)

We are not told how long the owner was gone, but we are told one day he did return, summoning his servants to do an audit of their books. We understand the owner had the right to do this: it was his money and they were servants, not owners of the money. The owner had a right to inspect what he expected.

What was the outcome? Verses 16-18 reveal to us that each servant acted in accordance with their lifestyle habits, validating the owner's expectations. The first two servants doubled the money. Obviously the owner expected the first servant to do the best and gave him the most money. He expected the second to do well. And he also expected the third – to not do so well, and gave him the least amount. It appears the master's expectations were not disappointed.

Our Audits

One thing we must always remember, there is accountability. The Kingdom lifestyle has woven into it accountability to our King and to each other.

Living in the Kingdom, we must grasp the truth that EVERTHING belongs to the King. He has given us the privilege to use His resources, but they are still his. This can be a challenge for us; we assume because I have them in my possession that means I own them. This is far from the truth.

Since these resources are the Kings, he has every right to do an audit of our stewardship. He has the right to inspect what He expects us to use them for.

The Rewards

After the audit, verses 21-28 tell us the rewards each servant received. From the context of the parable, we see that each servant reaped what they had sown: but it was the reward of the two faithful servants that is, at least to me, where it gets real exciting. So I will focus just on those two.

We are told the first two servants both doubled the money. Obviously they fulfilled the owner's expectations of responsibilities and he proceeds to reward them. It is the reward that is intriguing, exciting and applicable to us today.

So what was the reward given to these two faithful stewards? Not more money, but authority! Yes, more authority. We are told that the owner responded with: *"I will make thee ruler over many things" (Matthew 25:21, 23)*. The Bible In Basic English states it clearly: *"will give you control over great things."* The point I am making here is: it was their faithful stewardship of money that resulted in a greatly increased realm of authority.

Now, bring this into our modern context of living in Kingdom authority. Stewardship of His resources, specifically the money He has entrusted me with, will be a significant factor in determining how much spiritual authority I can be given. God's wealth is given to us for His purpose. When I faithfully use all the resources I possess: money, possessions and anything else in my control, I can expect Him to grant me a greater access to spiritual or Kingdom authority.

Parable of the Pounds

In Luke 19:12-26, we have a similar parable of an owner giving his servants *"pounds"* to use while he was away. While I will not go into all the details of this parable, it reveals the same truths. In this parable, the word *"pound"* is *mna* and means *"a Semitic word, both 'a weight' and 'a sum of money,' 100 shekels"* (Vine's). So again, we see that the servants received money that they were to use for their master's purpose. As with the parable of the talents, we find that two of the servants were faithful in their stewardship, doubling the money they had been entrusted with. As a result, their reward was more authority. In verses 17 & 19 we are told specifically their rewards were to *"have authority"* over a certain number of cities. Again, we see the principle: Faithful stewardship of money results in an increase of authority.

CHAPTER 10
THE STRONGHOLD OF RELIGIOUS TRADITION

We evangelicals are good at building rigid walls out of dogmatic stones...cemented together by the mortar of tradition. We erect these walls in systematic circles—then place within each our over-simplified, ultra inflexible "position." ~ Charles Swindoll

The scripture is clear about the authority that has been given to the church and to each believer. The Word has promised that believers would do greater works than those Jesus himself performed. Reviewing the early church, it is clearly seen that the apostles walked in a miracle producing authority. They performed the miraculous, and the Lord confirmed their preaching by signs and wonders. The Lord has further promised believers that we would receive power after His Spirit came upon us, and there would be miraculous signs that follow those that believe. This miraculous demonstration of Kingdom authority in the daily lives of the first believers was so powerful and convincing that cities were stirred to riots because of its affect, and a reverential fear or awe of God was produced with many souls being converted.

However, upon examining 21st century Christianity, it is apparent most churches are weak and anemic. There is little power evident in the daily lives of most of those calling themselves Christians. The "greater works" are not evident today as in the days of the first church. In the Christianity of today, we find that many of man's ideas have become a hindrance to the operation of the Spirit, limiting the church's ability to operate in Kingdom authority. Jesus said, *"Howbeit in vain do they worship me, teaching for doctrines the commandments of men. For laying aside the commandment of God, ye hold the tradition of men," (Mark 7:7-8)*. Jesus further spoke of the result of holding the traditions of man in verse 13, *"Making the word of God of none effect through your tradition, which ye have delivered:"* According to Thayer's *"Making of none effect"* is one word and it means *"deprive of force and authority."*

The greatest hindrance to Kingdom authority that is faced in this day and age is the tradition of men and the resulting structure of traditional churches. Traditions create a biased paradigm that is used to filter scripture. This tainted view of scripture affects the individual's faith and ability to walk in Kingdom authority. Centuries of man's tradition have created an organization that is far from the original church of sent (apostolic) believers.

Traditions can be a blessing or a curse. Many times traditions are a good reminder of who we are, of our heritage or identity. Paul speaking to the church at Thessalonica instructed them to: *"stand fast, and hold the traditions which ye have been taught, whether by word or our epistle" (2 Thessalonians 2:15)*. There are traditions that can be passed from one generation to another that can insure a continuation of purpose and being. This is obvious in the history of the Jewish nation. For many years, prior to 1948, they were a homeless people, yet they maintained their identity as a people.

However, there are times when traditions create a filter that colors how we view information or experiences of life. This way of seeing things becomes rigid and inflexible, causing a rejection of anything that does not blend with our traditional views. The traditions we are speaking of here are ONLY those that are of man's creation that HINDER the divine plan of God. In the New Testament, the Greek word translated as tradition or traditions is used thirteen times; only twice is it used in a positive manner.

Traditions can become strongholds of arguments, rationalizations or pretense that we use to justify a particular pattern of beliefs. Such statements as: "this is the way we've always done it," "if it was good enough for my parents, its good enough for me" or "we must maintain the old landmarks" all exhibit a tendency for maintaining strongholds. The problem with this thought process is that it can hinder the move of the Spirit of God. Jesus came to the religious leaders of Israel declaring by word and ministry who He was – the Messiah. Yet because of their religious traditions, the Pharisees missed Him.

Traditional Churches

The greatest hindrance to living in Kingdom authority and the church becoming truly apostolic (sent) is the battle we face with tradition. The traditional church is not necessarily one that has a specific distinguishable liturgical form or style. It is a church that operates with a particular man-made concept or intent of ministry that has been passed down, unquestioned, from generation to generation. Some traditions of church life have been passed on for centuries.

The full effect of how tradition can bind a church is revealed when the very word tradition is defined, both scripturally and secularly. According to Thayer's Greek Lexicon, Electronic Database, the Greek word translated tradition is *paradosis*, (Strong #3862).

- It is defined as: *"a giving over, giving up. 1. the act of giving up, the surrender: 2. a giving over which is done by word of mouth or in writing."*

- According to Merriam-Webster Online Dictionary; tradition's etymology is Middle English *tradicioun,* from Middle French & Latin; Middle French *tradition,* from Latin *tradition-, tradition and is the* action of handing over. It is from the same root word as treason. (emphasis added)

- Once again, according to Merriam-Webster Online Dictionary; the etymology of treason is Middle English *tresoun,* from Old French *traison,* from Latin *tradition-, traditio* act of handing over, from *tradere* to hand over, betray. (emphasis added)

It should be a shocking revelation to us that tradition and treason have the same etymology. They mean a handing over of something. So we see the significance of tradition is that it can be considered treason of beliefs or values that were once held by individuals or a group. In respect to the traditional church, we see that there has been a surrendering, a giving up or handing over of the power of God, as demonstrated through Kingdom authority. This treasonous act has been a replacing of the commandments and power of God for the traditions of men. This is truly making the commands of God none affect.

Digging a little deeper, we find that *paradosis* (tradition) is derived from *paradidomi* which has significant meanings for our discussion. According to Strong's it means, *"to surrender."* Thayer's states it is, *"to give over: properly, to give into the hands (of another) to give over into (one's) power or use: to deliver to one something to keep, use, take care of, manage."* The basic idea conveyed here is to surrender or to give over to the power of another. It is used 121 times in the New Testament and only 19 are used in a positive context.

Paul warns the church at Colossi of the potential dangers traditions have to spoil or enslave: *"Beware lest any man spoil you through philosophy and vain deceit, after the tradition* (paradosis) *of men, after the rudiments of the world, and not after Christ"*

(Colossians 2:8). The ISV puts it this way: *"See to it that no one enslaves you through philosophy and empty deceit according to human tradition."* The danger of man's religious traditions is they hold us captive or enslave us when they are held above the commandments of God.

Characteristics Of A Traditional Church

A review of modern Christianity and the traditional church will reveal to us the following characteristic of man's traditions that have developed in place of the Kingdom model.

Traditional churches are no longer preaching the gospel of the Kingdom, but are preaching a "bless me" gospel. This gospel is one that is focused primarily on how to make individuals feel better about themselves and their current life situations. This theme is the foundation of many sermons and ministries of the traditional church. Individuals attend to hear how they can be blessed in their lives, alleviating their pain and discomfort. The Word of God is used as a cookbook that is searched in an attempt to find the correct steps necessary to fix the current problem. Church attendance holds with little expectation of a life-altering encounter with Jesus Christ. Member's expectations focus on how they can be motivated, entertained, or shown how good God can make them and their lives. A casual look at much of the church growth literature reveals a focus on creating a church "mega store" or "mall" approach – find what the people are looking for and provide it for them. This type of gospel focus on salvation or the born again experience as the goal to be achieved. Once this happens, all that is required it to hold on, waiting until death or the return of Jesus Christ.

During a forty-five minute drive, this bless me gospel was so evident. A particular church sign I passed by read: "free trip to heaven, details inside". On the radio advertisement for a certain church, people were interviewed and asked why they went to church. The majority of comments were based on their perceived blessings: able to handle stress better, found relationships they were looking for, allowed them to get focused for the week. Yet another radio advertisement was promoting a particular ministry program. The focus of this ad was the destruction going on in the world and that life could end at any moment. The punch line was "are you ready?"

Unfortunately, this bless me gospel is setting individuals up for failure. The amount of blessings in our lives is used as an indicator of our spirituality. It is seen as the greater our faith, the greater our blessings will be. However, when needs are not met, there is the implication of a lack of faith or spirituality. Since life also contains heartache and pain, associating spirituality with blessings sets us up for disappointment, and eventually walking away from the church.

Because a traditional church has at its focus a "bless me" gospel, the majority of its resources are focused inward, towards keeping members happy and entertained. This results in many programs that are designed to attract the attention and interests of individuals. Unfortunately, many of these programs eventually loose their spiritual emphasis and degrade to social hours. A brief review of the church growth movement reveals fads of church growth methods that have been promoted, used, and then discarded as time passed. Many will hear of programs that are successful in attracting a crowd in a particular church. We get excited and we attempt to reproduce it. Some programs even attain such national notoriety that their originators create seminars on how to implement the programs. These may work at attracting crowds for a while, but when the newness or entertainment value wears off, and the crowds diminish because there is no spiritual depth, we seek yet another program to implement.

Because programs are the focus of a traditional church, there must be a staff, facilities, equipment, and there must be money! The largest segment of the budget is used to fund internal programs, buildings, and structure that are necessary to keep the programs functioning. The result is a vicious cycle; the programs need a building and money. Therefore to supply the money, more people are needed, which means more programs and more buildings and more money etc. You get the idea.

The traditional church continues the centuries-old division between the clergy and laity. There are designated, called or elected professionals who perform all ministry. In some settings, a select few of the laity are allowed to get involved. But for the most part, outside of boards of elders or deacons, we see the laity involvement at best, as Sunday School teachers and other ministries of helps.

This concept of a separation of clergy and laity is not new to the 21st century church. The apostle John records Jesus' words to us in regard to the ecclesiastical structure of the church at Pergamos.

> *And to the angel of the church in Pergamos write; ...But I have a few things against thee, ...So hast thou also them that hold the doctrine of the Nicolaitans, which thing I hate. (Revelation 2:12,14-15)*

To the church of Pergamos, the Lord speaks of His displeasure because they have them that *"hold the doctrine of the Nicolaitans"* which He hates. What is there about this particular doctrine that Jesus would hate?

The significance of this doctrine is found in the original Greek. *Nicolaitans* is the word: *Nikolaitees* or *Nikolaitou*, which means *"destruction of the people"* (Thayer's). This word is derived from *Nikolaos*; from NT:3534 and NT:2994; victorious over the people (Thayer's). The doctrine of the Nicolaitans was a conquering or victory over the people. It appears that this doctrine resulted in a great divide between the formal ministry and the laity, so much so that it was viewed as a conquering. This is far from the first century church where each member was a minister and the gospel was taken from house to house. The Lord hates the conquering of believers and the placing of ministry in the hands of a few.

Unfortunately, this structure results in power being centered in a select few. Historically, it has been shown that there have been continual power struggles within what was considered to be the church. Unfortunately, this structure produces a control issue for the leadership, resulting in the lack of a determined and planned method of training and equipping of the believers, fostering apathy among the members. If nothing is expected of the membership, nothing is what they will give. This structural division ignores the priesthood of believes, and wastes the gifting and talents God has placed in the body of believers. This is how we create believers who sit on the pew and hang on till they die or Jesus returns.

The traditional church is the greatest hindrance to the operation of Kingdom authority. It substitutes the structure, programs and mind of man for the will and miraculous demonstration of God. In contrast, the Kingdom focused church is one based on using the authority with which Jesus Christ has empowered believers. It is using this authority for His purpose the manner in which He desires, in the place they have been sent to.

Characteristics Of The Kingdom Focused Church

The Kingdom focused Church has as its purpose and goal to fill the earth with the image and glory of Jesus Christ. Just as God's intent from creation was that Adam was made in His image and commanded to fill the earth, the Kingdom focused Church is to raise up born again believers who are renewed after the image of the one who created them. These believers are then sent into the world declaring the kingdom of Heaven.

The Kingdom focused Church sees salvation, the born again experience, as an entrance into Kingdom work. Jesus came preaching that men were to repent because the kingdom of Heaven was at hand. To one religious leader, Jesus plainly stated that to see or enter the kingdom of Heaven, one must be born again of the water and the Spirit. This born again experience implies a new beginning, not an arrival at a destination. We are born again so we can see and enter the Kingdom. The proper perspective of heaven is that it is our reward for hearing *"well done, thou good and faithful servant, enter into your rest"(Matthew 25:21).*

The Kingdom focused church does not concentrate on the building of edifices or programs. It seeks the demonstration and propagation of the good news of Jesus Christ and His kingdom. The life of its members are to manifest the Kingdom of God daily. This is accomplished by recognizing the priesthood of every believer. Each believer is empowered by the Spirit, given a measure of gifting by the Spirit, and expected by the Spirit to use their giftings for the Kingdom purpose. It is the responsibility of the five-fold ascension gift ministries (apostles, prophets, evangelists, pastors and teachers) to equip the believers with knowledge in how to use their gifting for His glory. Part of this equipping is that once the believers are trained, they are sent out to use their giftings in the community. Therefore, the Kingdom focused Church's belief in the priesthood of all believers and the sending of the believers will result in a large portion of their resources being used outside the church facilities.

Summary

It is the Lord's desire to operate through His people, revealing Himself and His kingdom to a lost and hurting world. To do this, the church, His people, must examine their paradigm and remove those traditions of men, which are preventing the illumination of the truth of Kingdom authority. An illumination of the word of God to our minds and spirit will reveal some basic principles of apostolic authority that must be grasped by a transformed mind and acted upon by faith.

"That the God of our Lord Jesus Christ, the Father of glory, ***may give unto you the spirit of wisdom and revelation in the knowledge of him: The eyes of your understanding being enlightened;*** *that ye may know what is the hope of his calling, and what the riches of*

the glory of his inheritance in the saints," (Ephesians 1:17-18 emphasis added)

CHAPTER 11
MAKIN' IT REAL

The best evidence of our having the truth is our walking in the truth. ~ *Matthew Henry*

I firmly believe people have hitherto been a great deal too much taken up about doctrine and far too little about practice. The word "doctrine," as used in the Bible, means teaching of duty, not theory.
~ *George Macdonald*

Our walk counts far more than our talk, always!
~ *George Müller*

The goal of this chapter is to present a model of Kingdom lifestyle, one that is both practical and attainable. From this lifestyle, Kingdom opportunities will flow out of the average routines of daily life. The results: manifold opportunities to use the authority of the Kingdom, demonstrating its reality to this world.

In chapters two and three we established that as God's representatives we are bearers of His glory. Remember, glory is a form or appearance that attracts attention and brings recognition. It is our privilege to demonstrate the power of His presence in the routine rub of life causing others to recognize Him.

Now I know this all sounds good so far, but the question lingering either consciously or subconsciously is: "How can I do this in a practical way?" The simple answer is we must change our ideas from evangelistic actions and events to that of missionary or missional involvement in the micro-cultures we are ALREADY involved in.

The very nature of God is a sent one. He has taken the initiative to redeem and restore His creation. It is in our sentness (apostolic) that we, the church, become the instruments of God's mission. In short, God is on a mission of restoration and as born again believers, we are sent as his representatives to join him. You can obviously see how this fits with our first couple of chapters where we discussed our being sent as his image bearers.

However, it is not just about our going, but it is how we go. It is not enough to agree that we have been sent; the issue is how we demonstrate the Kingdom in our sentness. It should be our purpose to live out the Gospel in the context of the culture we have been sent to. We are to live a lifestyle demonstrating Kingdom authority in the midst of those who need the Gospel most.

Accomplishing this does not mean we add a bunch of meetings and events. Instead, we change the focus of our lives, learning to live out our daily activities with Gospel intentionality. We can be confident that God is already at work in the lives of those we touch.

The practical expression of this mindset is realizing that we are sent to reach a group of people. It may be a particular neighborhood, individuals connected to a specific activity, our work place or a certain group of professionals. This list is truly endless and is based on God using your individual circumstances and unique personality. Stop and examine the particular connections you already have, it could be here that the Lord is prompting you to serve.

Recognizing this, we should intentionally develop or deepen existing relationships. We should spend time, joining them in the routine or rhythms of life, seeking to incarnate Jesus and His kingdom by listening and serving. Ideally, we would join with a few others to best accomplish this.

Living this missionary lifestyle changes how we approach various aspects of our lives. It requires a re-aligning of such areas as: small gatherings, discipleship, understanding the rhythms of life, opening our homes and working with those on the fringes. The following are some ideas for practical expression of this lifestyle.

Small Gatherings

In practical terms, to go, means we must move our interaction from just Sunday gatherings to a place society sees as neutral. An effective means of this is small, informal gatherings where spiritual conversations and Bible discussions are encouraged.

Now before you freak out and say you can't teach a bible study, I am not advocating a formal teacher/student type format. It could be better described as a journey of bible discovery. This context has a facilitator who keeps the group focused, but everyone has input. It should be simple, regular and focus on the story of God and His kingdom. We should study to discover our part in His story. Focus alone should not be on how we can grow in the word, but learning more of His mission and how we are to join Him in transforming our immediate world.

Discipleship

Grasping His mission of redemption and restoration reveals to us the purpose of Kingdom demonstration is to make disciples. Jesus instructed the disciples to go and make disciples and to teach them to obey the things that he commanded. Discipleship is not reproducing some great preacher or bible teacher, which sets standard too high. It is reproducing those who are striving to live like Jesus, simply communicating the story of God and the good news of His kingdom.

Rhythms

Ok, so how do we do this practically? We learn to live the rhythms of our life on purpose, expecting God to provide the opportunity to demonstrate His kingdom to those around us. Stop and think about it, our lives already have a rhythm.

We all have our daily work or school routines. We stop at the same Starbucks or gas station for our morning coffee, as we drive the same route. If we have children, there are sporting or extracurricular events to attend. We have our grocery and laundry days and we frequent the same restaurants. It is in the midst of these rhythms we come into contact with those who Jesus is on mission to introduce into His kingdom.

It is not necessary for us to add extra events, but to take the time to seek Him and how he wants us to be aware of those around us in our normal rhythms. It is during these times He will prod us to be obedient and demo His kingdom. Each scenario is so unique that I could not begin to describe how He could and would use you in an individual's life. But let me give you one small personal example from my life.

I love coffee and coffee shops, especially Starbucks. At this time, I live a couple blocks from a Starbucks and it has become one of my hangouts. I have made it a point to learn some of the barista's names and their stories. On one particular day, I said a quick prayer, asking the Lord to show me where someone was responding to His work. On that day, I went to Starbucks and immediately, a barista strikes up a spiritual conversation and we were off. While we were talking another one walks by and exclaims, "I knew you were a Christian!" I asked her why she thought that. She replied: "There is such a spirit of peace around you." There is no reason for her to have made that statement, except, God is at work in her life and I intentionally seek involvement in the lives of others during the normal rhythms of my daily life!

The point is He desires us to live out our identity (really His) in every day ways!

Open House

The bible says much about hospitality. This is not some ministry or program that greets the guest on Sunday. It is a lifestyle that is to be exhibited to the world. A casual glance at scripture reveals that both in the Old and New Testaments, the common practice was to open the home to others. At the birth of the church in Acts, hospitality was readily evident in the lives of the believers. The following text is commonly quoted, but should not lose its significance:

> *They joined with the other believers and devoted themselves to the apostles' teaching and fellowship, sharing in the Lord's Supper and in prayer...And all the believers met together constantly and shared everything they had. They sold their possessions and shared the proceeds with those in need. They worshiped together at the Temple each day, met in homes for the Lord's Supper, and shared their meals with great joy and generosity -- (Acts 2:42, 44-46)*

In short, what we see happening here is the early disciples opened their homes and lives to others.

Now I admit, this is probably the most challenging aspect of living in Kingdom authority. We like our privacy. We feel the home is our castle, our place of refuge. It is my place to let my hair down (obviously speaking proverbial for me!), why would I want anyone to invade my space?

The answer: some aspects of discipleship are not taught, but caught. We can give bible studies and handouts on the principles of relationships, marriage, raising children, success in life and so on. Yet sometimes the greatest lesson is real life demonstration. This is what happens when we open our homes, it is in the normal routines of life when others can see us model what we teach.

Focusing On The Fringe

We find that Jesus hung out with those shunned by the religious society. It was common for him to be seen in the company of publicans and sinners. He was kind to the adulteress and actually touched societies' untouchables, the leper.

One evening, Matthew invited Jesus to a party. The other guests were tax collectors and the New Living Translation states *"notorious sinners."* The response of the religious Pharisees was to question why Jesus would *"eat with such scum?"* (NLT) Jesus responded: *"Healthy people don't need a doctor -- sick people do."* (Matthew 9:12)

This text seems to imply that those that need to see the greatness of our King and kingdom are those who are on the margins of society. They are the disenfranchised and castaway, the "lower" class, the homeless etc. These individuals do not want to be someone's project: they need more than a program of handouts. What they desire is acceptance and inclusion into our lives.

Grasping our sentness as the image bearer and representatives of Jesus, it should change the intent of our daily routines. Life does not have to be a series of ruts, trudging along, waiting for the weekend and a spiritually high event. **Viewing the rhythms of life as opportunities to contextualize in a tangible way the power of the Gospel and our King gives each day a purpose!** When we are intentionally seeking His mission daily: at work, school, recreation, hanging out etc, we will find He presents the opportunity for us to demonstrate His kingdom! It is our privilege to provide the foretaste of His kingdom here and now!

Practical Kingdom Revealing Steps

So now that our minds have been stretched, what are some practical things we can do to begin living this type of lifestyle? The following is an article revealing eight steps that are already part of our lifestyles. By changing our intent, we can now make them opportunities for Kingdom manifestation.

8 Ways to Easily Be Missional
Jonathan K. Dodson
http://www.churchplantingnovice.wordpress.com/

1. Eat with Non-Christians.
We all eat three meals a day. Why not make a habit of sharing one of those meals with a non-Christian or with a family of non-Christians? Go to lunch with a co-worker, not by yourself. Invite the neighbors over for family dinner. If it's too much work to cook a big dinner, just order pizza and put the focus on conversation. When you go out for a meal invite others. Or take your family to family-style restaurants where you can sit at the table with strangers and strike up conversation. Cookout and invite Christians and non-Christians. Flee the Christian subculture.

2. Walk, Don't Drive.
If you live in a walkable area, make a practice of getting out and walking around your neighborhood, apartment complex, or campus. Instead of driving to the mailbox, convenience store, or apartment office, walk to get mail, groceries, and stuff. Be deliberate in your walk. Say hello to people you don't know. Strike up conversations. Attract attention by walking the dog, taking a 6-pack (and share), bringing the kids. Make friends. Get out of your house! Take interest in your neighbors. Ask questions. Pray as you go. Save some gas, the planet, and some people.

3. Be a Regular.
Instead of hopping all over the city for gas, groceries, haircuts, eating out, and coffee, go to the same places. Get to know the staff.

Go to the same places at the same times. Smile. Ask questions. Be a regular. I have friends at coffee shops all over the city. My friends at Starbucks donate a ton of left over pastries to our church 2-3 times a week. We use them for church gatherings and occasionally give to the homeless. Build relationships. Be a Regular.

4.   Hobby with Non-Christians.
Pick a hobby that you can share. Get out and do something you enjoy with others. Try City League sports. Local rowing and cycling teams. Share your hobby by teaching lessons. Teach sewing lessons, piano lessons, violin, guitar, knitting, tennis lessons. Be prayerful. Be intentional. Be winsome. Have fun. Be yourself.

5.   Talk to Your Co-workers.
How hard is that? Take your breaks with intentionality. Go out with your team or task force after work. Show interest in your co-workers. Pick four and pray for them. Form mom groups in your neighborhood and don't make them exclusively Christian. Schedule play dates with the neighbors' kids. Work on mission.

6.   Volunteer with Non-Profits.
Find a non-profit in your part of the city and take Saturday a month to serve your city. Bring your neighbors, your friends, or your small group. Spend time with your church serving your city. Once a month. You can do it!

7.   Participate in City Events.
Instead of playing X-Box, watching TV, or surfing the net, participate in city events. Go to fundraisers, festivals, clean-ups, summer shows, and concerts. Participate missionally. Strike up conversation. Study the culture. Reflect on what you see and hear. Pray for the city. Love the city. Participate with the city.

8. Serve your Neighbors.
Help a neighbor by weeding, mowing, building a cabinet, fixing a car. Stop by the neighborhood association or apartment office and ask if there is anything you can do to help improve things. Ask your local Police and Fire Stations if there is anything you can do to help them. Get creative. Just serve!

God is on a mission to restore what was lost at Adam's rebellion. To do so, he is seeking to restore mankind back to the place Adam originally had: God's image and likeness on the earth. The vehicle that God chooses to bring the good news of restoration is his church: the body of born again, Kingdom living believers. It is this group of people, "taking it to the streets," that will join God on his mission. The Kingdom lifestyle is one that uniquely demonstrates His power to this world, making his Kingdom attractive and results in discipleship development.

CHAPTER 12
HIS WORD CONFIRMED

True disciples are those who go beyond simply believing. They act out their belief. ~ James E. Faust

It has been my privilege for the last 6 plus years (at the time of this writing) to see the Lord confirm this word of Living In Kingdom Authority. Since being commissioned to minister these truths, I have seen more of the miraculous power of God demonstrated, than in my prior 24 years of living for Him. In the next few pages, I want to give you some of the testimonies of His mighty works. I trust they will increase your faith.

One Sunday, during our pastorate in south Georgia, a member informed me of her recent doctors visit. It seems they believed she had a problem with the valves of her heart and connected her to a portable monitor for a week of observation. During worship service we prayed for her, speaking with authority to the heart condition. The following Monday, she reported that the doctor called her saying she did not need to wear the monitor because she did not have a heart problem!

On another Sunday, a member came to church protectively cradling her arm, which she was unable to lift. She stated that the doctor had diagnosed a pinched nerve. During service, we prayed for her, speaking with authority over the pinched nerve. Then we instructed her to lift her arms. She steadily lifted her arms and then with joy, began to wave them about in worship!

On a trip to Europe, at the conclusion of our teaching series, I had individuals pray for each other. Unbeknownst to me, one lady went and shut herself in the restroom. Later, she told me that she thought to herself, "If this is true, I don't need someone to pray for me, I can pray for myself!" So while in the restroom, she laid hands on her knees and spoke with authority to the rheumatoid arthritis and instantly the pain was gone! But, just to make sure, she waited a week till the next service to testify of her healing. She told me, "I wanted to make sure it was real!" Yes it is real!

Also, during this trip, there was another man with arthritis in his hands. As someone prayed for him, speaking with authority, he reported that the pain left and the swelling went away.

One weekend, I was ministering at a men's retreat for a local church. I did not teach the full series of Living In Kingdom Authority, just one message on faith and speaking with authority. At the conclusion of the message, I had the men pray for each other. It was at this time that the Lord healed many. One man testified that as he was prayed for, the pain in his arthritic knees left.

There was another man who had been diagnosed with thoracic outlet syndrome. This resulted in a decreased blood flow to his hand and numbness. As he was prayed for, instantly his hand warmed and the numbness left. The following morning at service, he stated that for the first time in years he was able to sleep lying on that shoulder.

Again, at this same retreat, there was a man who had difficulty turning his head from side to side. During the prayer time, he grabbed his neck and took authority over the issue. He reported that immediately, he was able to turn his head from side to side.

On one occasion, I had the privilege of being a keynote speaker at a conference in Cape Town, South Africa. The morning following my first session, Doug (a pastor friend who traveled with me) and I were sitting quietly having coffee and some cookies for breakfast. There was a local pastor who knew I was a doctor and approached me about his shoulder problem. We discussed some of the possible diagnosis and I gave him a couple of suggestions. Then I said, "Or, if you believe Jesus can heal you, we will pray for you." He blurted out, "I believe!" At this time, Doug and I stood up and laid our hands on his shoulder and quietly spoke with authority to the shoulder issue. When we were finished, I asked him "How's your shoulder?" He then began to lift his arm hesitantly, until he came to the place it used to hurt. Then he lifted it above his head and began waving it around, declaring, "It doesn't hurt!"

I have ministered twice in the Philippines: I love the worship of the Filipino people! On both of these occasions, God demonstrated His power. During one service, two individuals testified of having their once blurred vision restored to normal. I still have a photo of one lady weeping with raised hands as she praised God for her healing. On another occasion, I taught our series at a local bible school. During this time two of the missionaries were healed: one of a shoulder problem and the other of a low back issue.

After returning home from this trip, the missionary emailed me with a testimony from two of the students. They told the story that while they were helping a pastor in one of the mountainous areas; they came upon a man that "could not move his limbs." They stated that they spoke with authority and that the man could "immediately move his limbs!" Let me add, this is the whole purpose of our teaching, that when we leave, others will take the truths back to their homes and begins to step out in faith and demonstrate Jesus and his kingdom!

While ministering in a church in Illinois, at the end of our series, when individuals prayed for each other the following happened: two were healed of COPD - their breathing became normal, one with sciatic pain healed and another with arthritic hip pain gone. Also at this meeting, there was one individual who came up to me holding his hearing aid reporting that his hearing was now normal!

In a south Georgia church, when individuals prayed for each other God confirmed his word by healing a man who had not been able to straighten his hand. An individual who could not stand and was told they needed surgery was now standing pain free!

In a south Missouri service, a woman with an inguinal hernia was prayed for and healed. It was exciting to watch her feel all around her abdomen attempting to find where it had been!

On a trip to Japan, one of the missionaries was experiencing sever foot pain which was obvious by his dramatic limp. After the saints prayed, speaking with authority, he was dancing and shouting with no pain and the limp was gone!

During another trip to Japan, in a midweek bible study, an elderly Okinawan lady asked for payer for hip pain. Again, we spoke with authority over the problem. She bowed and thanked us quietly. As we continued that week with the conference, I watched her walk. At the end of the conference, many of us were sitting at a restaurant and I asked her about her hip. With a wave of her hand she replied: "The pain was gone as soon as you prayed!"

While in Pakistan, I was ministering at a pastor's conference. I noticed there was an elder pastor, using a cane, limping as he moved around the group. Between sessions, he asked me to pray for his back and hip. Quietly and calmly, I took authority and spoke healing. He politely thanked me and walked off. As I watched him the rest of the conference, he began to carry the cane, and then walked more briskly and ultimately, he was dancing before the Lord in worship. I later asked him about his back and his comment was "the pain left as soon as you prayed!"

Most of the time, I teach the Living In Kingdom Authority series to larger assemblies or in conferences. On one occasion, I taught a weekly series to a small study group. During the next to the last session (prior to the lesson when I have the believers demonstrate) there was a young lady who could not lift her arm without shoulder pain. So I took this opportunity to give them simple instructions on how to speak with authority. I very simply laid my hand on her shoulder, as the others joined me, and took authority over her shoulder problem. It was mildly humorous to me as after about 20-30 seconds I was finished and stood watching the others continue in a traditional manner of prayer: asking God to heal. After about a minute of this, they noticed I was done and they quit. At this time, I asked the young lady to lift her arm past the point where it previously hurt. With excitement she lifted it pain free and a full range of motion. A week later, she was still pain free.

I trust you will sense the spirit in which I give these testimonies. I have been so privileged to be His voice with this message of Kingdom authority. Nothing that has happened is because of anything I have done or am worthy of: **it is all Jesus!**

These testimonies have been given for three reasons.
- First, to give Jesus glory!
- Second, to show that this is not theory, but it is experiential.
- Third, to build your faith that Jesus wants to use you!

I trust these words have done that and you will now step out and become His representative.

CONCLUSION

(The church) It was and is the chosen instrument of God to expand his kingdom. ~ *Reggie McNeal*

In Genesis we observe that the Lord created a universe and the earth with the sole purpose of filling them with His image and glory. To accomplish this, Adam was created in God's image and given dominion over His creation. The next instruction was that he should be fruitful, multiply and replenish the earth, filling creation with the image and likeness of God himself. Unfortunately, Adam failed in this mission, necessitating that the Lord would begin a process to redeem fallen man and restore His image to creation.

Jesus Christ came as the last Adam to restore what had been lost by the first Adam, dominion and the image of God on earth. As God who had come in the flesh, His first message was; *"Repent: for the kingdom of heaven is hand."* (Matthew 4:17) This bold declaration of the Lord revealed that the authority and dominion of heaven had returned to mankind.

The first command of this declaration was repent or change your way of thinking and living because the kingdom of Heaven is at hand. He was issuing a wake up call to those bound by the traditions of men. Even more important than this, He was expressing an inward desire that individuals would change how they were thinking and begin to live life from a Kingdom view. It was His desire for His people to become what they were created for; to reveal the image of an invisible God to the world.

It is still His desire today that we should reveal a glorious image to creation. The church, as the body of Christ, is to continue the work He restored by His death, burial and resurrection. The church is to be powerful, exercising a heavenly authority here on this earth. Our services and teaching should not be weak, but filled with power from on high.

The Vision Of The Church

Jesus stated: *"I will build my church; and the gates of hell shall not prevail against it." (Matthew 16:18)* The Apostle of our faith could issue such powerful word because He is the source of all authority and dominion. Since it is His church, He desires it to be a powerful, victorious demonstration of the kingdom of Heaven here on earth. Just as Adam was given dominion and expected to fill the earth with God's image, we as members of His body are called, empowered and sent with the same purpose – to fill this world with the image of Jesus Christ.

> *And he gave some, apostles; and some, prophets; and some, evangelists; and some, pastors and teachers; For the perfecting of the saints, for the work of the ministry, for the edifying of the body of Christ: Till we all come in the unity of the faith, and of the knowledge of the Son of God, unto a perfect man, unto the measure of the stature of the fulness of Christ: (Ephesians 4:11-13)*

To prepare the church to accomplish His plan, gifts were given to equip the church. These gifts are the ministry of the apostle, prophet, evangelists, pastors and teachers. It is the purpose

Conclusion

of these ministries to instruct and equip the individual members of the church in the operation of their individual gifts and the use of Kingdom authority. I believe the church that Jesus sees is one where each member walks in Kingdom authority. As members grasp their giftedness, they are sent into the body to use their measure of gifting to build up the body.

When members exhibit the faith to walk in their giftedness, the Lord's image will be revealed and the power of the Kingdom will be demonstrated. Miraculous signs and wonders will be seen because He will confirm His word. People will see Jesus Christ in a way that they have never seen Him before. This is when we will see the kingdom of Heaven manifest in the daily lives of His people. This is when we will begin to see His will done on earth as it is in heaven. He will no longer be a historical figure or the center of a philosophy or a religion. But, by the actions of those who are walking in Kingdom authority, He will become real to the world.

It is our desire to participate with you as the Lord reveals His place for you in the operation of Kingdom authority. Since we have begun to follow His leading and associate ourselves with those who are being used in Kingdom authority, we have witnessed the miraculous. There have been those healed of: heart problems, pinched nerves, knee injuries, goiters, vision restored, lame walking, growths disappeared and so many more. Praise the Lord!

This miraculous manifestation is not for a few, but it is for each and every believer who is willing to answer the call. It is to those who are willing to step out in faith, following the leading of Jesus. This is for you, born again child of God!

About Dr Martin Schmaltz

Dr. Martin's passion is to see Jesus manifested in the lives of each believer as they live a lifestyle of Kingdom authority. In his 17 years of ministry, as a pastor and itinerant teacher, he has experienced the transformation from traditional Christianity to Kingdom illumination. During this time, he has seen Jesus manifest his power and presence in mighty ways. Many have been healed, delivered and empowered to walk in Kingdom authority.

Today, Dr. Martin is challenging the traditional paradigm of church and enlightening the body of believers to the potential that lies within them. Much of his time is spent ministering the principles of Living In Kingdom Authority and re-alignment of the New Testament church structure. He travels frequently overseas and has ministered in: Pakistan, The Netherlands, Okinawa Japan, Swaziland Africa, Cape Town South Africa, Philippines and the Kingdom of Tonga. It is his desire to create a strategic network of individuals whose purpose is to manifest Jesus and His kingdom through the body of Christ.

Dr. Martin is available to speak to your local assembly, organization or ministry.

The focus of this ministry is revealing the truths of the word of God that empower the priesthood of believers. The result is a greater level of faith to demonstrate the miraculous: translating into the potential for a greater harvest.

Some message titles and topics available are:
- Living In Kingdom Authority (series)
- The Attractional Lifestyle Of The Kingdom (series)
- The Nature And Structure Of Strongholds
- Becoming A Son of God
- Possessing The Faith Of God
- The Priesthood Of Believers

- The Church
- Ministry gifts: their discovery and operation (series)
- The structure and function of the five fold ministry
- Defining biblical community
- The necessity of New Testament church structure

For more ministry information visit the following web links:
- Website, www.martinschmaltz.com, for more articles that Empower, Challenge & Reimage Church.

- A free MP3 sermon, "Defining Apostolic." The first in our series of "Apostolic Authority, Every Believer's Privilege." http://bit.ly/aVW54c

Also By Dr. Martin Schmaltz

But God, You Promised What's Happening When Nothing's Happening

The purpose of "But God, You Promised…" is to connect with the heart of believers who are experiencing a "silent" God in the midst of a wilderness wandering, waiting for their promise to materialize. It is a peek into His process of development: when it appears nothing is happening, is when everything is happening.

By examining the life of Joseph, we will see that it can be the very word from the Lord that becomes the instrument of our purification and development. It is in this long wilderness time that our character and skills are developed, preparing us for the fulfillment of His promise.

But God, You Promised… is to nudge your faith, encouraging you to keep on keepin' on! God has you right where he wants you!

View sampler here: http://martinschmaltz.com/products/book-but-god-you-promised/

Bibliography

The following is a list of Biblical Resources referenced through this work. These were accessed through PC Study Bible, Version 4.2B, www.Biblesoft.com, Copyright c 1988-2004.

(Strong's) - Biblesoft's New Exhaustive Strong's Numbers and Concordance with Expanded Greek-Hebrew Dictionary. Copyright © 1994, 2003 Biblesoft, Inc. and International Bible Translators, Inc.

(Vine's) - from Vine's Expository Dictionary of Biblical Words, Copyright (c)1985, Thomas Nelson Publishers

(Thayer's) - from Thayer's Greek Lexicon, Electronic Database. Copyright © 2000, 2003 by Biblesoft, Inc. All rights reserved.

(Holman) - from Holman Bible Dictionary. (c) Copyright 1991 by Holman Bible Publishers. All rights reserved.

NAS Exhaustive Concordance of the Bible with Hebrew-Aramaic and Greek Dictionaries Copyright © 1981, 1998 by The Lockman Foundation

(ISBE) - International Standard Bible Encyclopaedia, Electronic Database Copyright (c)1996 by Biblesoft

(Nelson's) - Nelson's Illustrated Bible Dictionary, Copyright (c)1986, Thomas Nelson Publishers

McClintock and Strong Encyclopedia, Electronic Database. Copyright (c) 2000 by Biblesoft

Vincent's Word Studies in the New Testament, Electronic Database. Copyright (c) 1997 by Biblesoft

Dictionary of Jesus and the Gospels © 1992 by InterVarsity Christian Fellowship/USA. All rights reserved.

Dictionary of Paul and His Letters © 1993 by InterVarsity Christian Fellowship/USA.

(TWOT) Theological Wordbook of the Old Testament. Copyright (c) 1980 by The Moody Bible Institute of Chicago

Other Resources
Lexical Aids To The New Testament, The Hebrew-Greek Key Study Bible, AMG Publishers

Dictionary.com. Collins English Dictionary - Complete & Unabridged 10th Edition. HarperCollins Publishers.

HELPS[TM] Word-studies, copyright 1987, 2011 by Help Ministries, Inc. For complete text and additional resources visit: HelpsBible.com

www.ingramcontent.com/pod-product-compliance
Lightning Source LLC
Chambersburg PA
CBHW071703040426
42446CB00011B/1887